INDIA & PAKISTAN

Path Towards 21st Century

By Dr. Ira Yadav

Gaurav Book Centre Pvt. Ltd.
Delhi

Publisher
GAURAV BOOK CENTRE PVT LTD
4832/24,Prahlad Lane,S-207 Ansari
Road, Daryaganj, Delhi-110002
Ph.: 43570976, 23278261
Email: gauravbookcentre@gmail.com

Edition: 2015

ISBN: 978-93-83316-21-2

Laser Typesetting
JEE-VEE Graphics, Delhi

Price: 595/-

Printed
Vikas Computers, Delhi

Preface

India Pakistan Relations is one of the hall marks of the success of the foreign policies in India and Pkaistan. There was lot of hues that Modi Regime will refix the Pakistan Syndrome. India is likely to adopt a "wait and see" attitude. While the election of a new government may have elevated resolve to punish Pakistan in case of a terrorist attack, it has not increased India's capacity to coerce its neighbor into any specific outcome.

Awarding the MFN status to India is important in its own right. A substantial part of the business community, in particular small- and medium-sized enterprises, seem to fear being overwhelmed by a massive arrival of cheaper Indian products on the Pakistani market. The main political parties support Sharif's policy. Jihadi organizations, on the contrary, oppose any trade deals with New Delhi as long as Kashmir remains under Indian control.

Awarding the MFN status to India would thus serve the interests of the civilian government, not to mention the country, whose economy would benefit from free trade with India. But such a move would only partly benefit the military. This relative convergence opens some diplomatic and political space that the government can exploit, providing it can keep its relations with the military under control. Yet, a spectacular advance in trade relations between India and Pakistan is unlikely. In the delay, Pakistan, whose economy is in shambles, has much more to lose than India does. New Delhi can afford patience. Its economic future lies in its integration in the global economy, not in any specific trade relation with its South Asian neighbors.

Contents

Introduction

India Pakistan Relations is one of the hall marks of the success of the foreign policies in India and Pkaistan. There was lot of hues that Modi Regime will refix the Pakistan Syndrome. There is also appreehension that Pakistan will also be squeezed under the Modi Wave. It might be possible that the new beginning of hostility will occur. There is no doubt there are many factors which use this opprtunity to pick up to dismantle the breathing speace between the two countries.

India is likely to adopt a "wait and see" attitude. While the election of a new government may have elevated resolve to punish Pakistan in case of a terrorist attack, it has not increased India's capacity to coerce its neighbor into any specific outcome. New Delhi will have to walk a fine line between ignoring Pakistan, which it can't control and does not need economically, and keeping the door to better relations open enough to provide a real incentive for Islamabad to adopt meaningful new policies—all without making unilateral concessions to Pakistan.

A year ago, then-candidate Sharif made the normalization of relations with India a central plank of his platform. Hopes were high, therefore, that Pakistan would finally extend India Most-Favored-Nation (MFN) status, removing tariff and other trade barriers. Sharif did not spell out any preconditions. But, twelve months later, the issue is still pending. Pakistan is now stipulating that the MFN status will be attributed to India only if New Delhi reopens the composite dialogue, a stalled executive-level negotiation process.

Awarding the MFN status to India is important in its own right. A substantial part of the business community, in particular small- and medium-sized enterprises, seem to fear being overwhelmed by a massive arrival of cheaper Indian products on the Pakistani market. Nontariff barriers to India's market have also been invoked as a justification for Pakistan's hesitations.

Yet, the Pakistani government continues to insist on the need to facilitate bilateral trade between the two countries. It blames several Indian lobbies (the automobile, textile and pharmaceutical industries as well as the agricultural lobbies) for obstructing the negotiations and maintains that awarding India MFN status would benefit Pakistan.

However, the MFN issue provides clues to a larger domestic political dynamic in Pakistan. The main political parties support Sharif's policy. Jihadi organizations, on the contrary, oppose any trade deals with New Delhi as long as Kashmir remains under Indian control. Here, as elsewhere, the jihadis are joined by the military—whose opposition Sharif seems to have underestimated. The nomination of Raheel Sharif as replacement for Ashfaq Parvez Kayani as Chief of Army Staff (COAS) did not usher a more receptive posture in Rawalpindi. It was the military that insisted that the government take the small- and medium-sized enterprises' objections to heart. It also lent its explicit support to their cause, warning the Sharif brothers "against making rapid concessions, particularly in the run-up to India's general election." In February 2014, Shabaz Sharif, the prime minister's brother, obliquely accused the military of obstructing trade normalization.

Awarding the MFN status to India would thus serve the interests of the civilian government, not to mention the country, whose economy would benefit from free trade with India. But such a move would only partly benefit the military. This relative convergence opens some diplomatic and political space that the government can exploit, providing it can keep its relations with the military under control. Yet, a spectacular advance in trade relations between India and Pakistan is unlikely. In the delay, Pakistan, whose economy is in shambles, has much more to lose than India does. New Delhi can afford patience. Its economic future lies in its integration in the global economy, not in any specific trade relation with its South Asian neighbors.

The Kashmir Dispute

The situation in Kashmir can be explained from a similar civil-military perspective. The Pakistani army is in no position to challenge India along the Line of Control (LoC) that divides Kashmir, since the bulk of its forces are positioned on its western front. The Pakistan military seems bent on curbing any temptation by the civilian government to rush into a detente. To stave it off, it provokes India, to make rapprochement politically difficult on that side of the border.

Skirmishes in Jammu and Kashmir resumed in August 2013, shortly after the Chief of Army Staff (COAS) told the newly elected prime minister that rapprochement with India was acceptable, but should not proceed too quickly. But the incidents remained limited, so as to avoid any escalation. The appointment of a new COAS, Raheel Sharif, did not alter the military's position on Kashmir.

The military's hardening of its position on Kashmir did not prevent Nawaz Sharif from attending Modi's swearing in, but the predictable absence of tangible results on the Kashmir issue after Sharif's trip to New Delhi was used by the military and its allies to attack the prime minister on his return to Pakistan.

A serious escalation in the military buildup on either side of the LoC is unlikely. The significance of the Kashmir issue does seem to be changing, however. Kashmir has become as much an indicator of the evolution of civil-military relations in Pakistan as of the Indian-Pakistani relationship. But this evolution does not make a settlement of the issue any less complex and uncertain than it was in the past.

Indian Perspectives and Options

For India, the primary question is far less about Islamabad's irredentist claims on its territory than about the uncertainty of Pakistan's political future. For many Indian officials across the political spectrum, the lack of a unified Pakistani center of power with a single policy makes meaningful negotiation and settlements impossible. India is, therefore, condemned to remain essentially reactive until Pakistan can resolve the tensions in its foreign policy. True, New Delhi can favor or close any possibility of dialogue. It can also raise the cost of potential aggression. But it cannot coerce Pakistan into any peace agreement against Islamabad's will. The decision to normalize the relationship belongs ultimately to Pakistan.

There is real anxiety in New Delhi about the possibility that Pakistan's security establishment may be tempted to test the new Indian government. In a recent article, journalist Praveen Swami enumerated five possible Indian responses to an attack originating in Pakistan: doing nothing, coercion through Indian-army mobilization along the LoC and the international border, strikes on jihadist training camps, using artillery and infantry along the LoC, and the use of covert means.

None of these options, however, are totally satisfactory. Calculated inaction, for example, characterized New Delhi's response to the Lashkar-e-Taiba attacks in Mumbai in November 2008. This approach earned India goodwill with major powers and brought pressure to bear against Pakistan. No major Lashkar-e-Taiba attack on Indian territory has taken place since then. But even though a restrained strategy paid dividends in 2008, it is highly dependent on third parties, such as the United States.

Similarly, coercion modeled on India's 2001-2002 response to the Pakistani-sponsored attack against the Indian parliament, has its drawbacks. India coerced Pakistan into mobilizing its forces along the international border. This response weakened Pakistan's economy, but also proved very costly for New Delhi. Limited strikes on Pakistani jihadist training camps or shelling targets across the LoC are also possible options, but it is uncertain whether they would produce meaningful results and they carry a high risk of escalation, up to and including the use of nuclear weapons.

The best guarantee of stability lies, therefore, in Pakistan's exercising restraint due to its domestic-security situation. The intensification of terrorist attacks on Pakistani soil compels Islamabad to reduce its force levels along the LoC and the international border, heightening its disadvantage vis-à-vis the Indian military and forcing Pakistan to exercise greater caution.

The Modi government will have to define a level of engagement with Pakistan that is sufficient to prevent the temptation of sponsoring terrorism, but limited enough to force Islamabad to make real concessions in antiterrorism to secure greater gains. Should New Delhi make significant concessions early in the process, the incentive to renounce terrorism as a way of achieving foreign-policy objectives will be nil or limited. The continuation of the back-channel negotiations that walk this fine line could offer, once more, the most effective instrument in advancing the relationship.

Rivalry in Afghanistan

But even back-channel negotiations are unlikely to prevent the rivalry from playing out once again in Afghanistan. With the departure of U.S. forces slated for the end of 2016 at the latest, chances are that Afghanistan will again become the backdrop for a proxy conflict because few core interests on either side would be at stake, thus diminishing the risk of a nuclear escalation.

Both sides deny this possibility. Pakistani officials keep claiming that the era of interfering in its northern neighbor's internal affairs is over. As evidence of such ostensibly responsible behavior, Islamabad has reached out to its erstwhile foes from the former Northern Alliance, facilitated a reconciliation process between the Taliban and the Afghan government, and cooperated in the Afghan elections, assuring everyone that it did not support any particular group. Some believe, however, that Pakistan is still trying to promote the emergence of an Afghan government it can influence or control, and expedite the return of Afghan refugees to prevent their potentially violent involvement in Pakistani politics. What Pakistan presents as a wholesale reversal of its old strategy is merely a tactical readjustment designed to meet changing realities on the ground. Interference is still a reality, despite some genuine rethinking in some government circles.

The participation of the Taliban in the Afghan government (or their control of some provinces) is antithetical to New Delhi's primary goals of preventing the return of the Taliban to power, while also weakening the connection between the Taliban and the Pakistani security establishment. To thwart such an outcome, New Delhi has established around Afghanistan a quasicontainment policy with all of Kabul's neighbors except Pakistan, and unfailingly supports the Afghan government.

But the announced U.S withdrawal will inevitably weaken India's position. New Delhi knows that its support to Kabul will at best slow down the erosion of the government authority. More importantly, the political chaos or even simply the additional tensions that could possibly result from the accusations of fraud in the second round of Afghanistan's elections will further diminish the legitimacy of the next government at a time when the insurgency is showing a new vigor in the east and the south of the country. So far, Pakistan's preoccupation with anti-Islamabad militants offers India the best protection against excessive interference in its Afghanistan affairs, but it makes New Delhi dependent on a situation it does not control.

Although India and Pakistan officially profess their goodwill towards one another, none of the conditions for a real rapprochement are met. Despite Pakistan's assurances that it is ready to seek an agreement with Modi, as it did under the last BJP government, the consensus between civilian and military is only superficial. It would, however, be a mistake to assume that the military is resolutely opposed to all kinds of rapprochement with India. The military still needs the civilian government to break the vicious cycle of economic regression and international isolation in which successive governments (including military regimes) and adventurist policies of the security establishment have locked up the country. It therefore wants the prime minister to improve relations with New Delhi in service of that goal, but to do so without creating the kind of organic links that would emerge from the development of a strong economic relationship. Moreover, peace with India would challenge the narrative that the military's outsized role in Pakistani government and society is essential to the country's security, and would, therefore, seriously challenge its influence on Pakistani politics.

Still, it is clear that the military is no longer politically omnipotent. The relative unity of the mainstream political parties on the issue of noncooperation with the military limits the latter's capacity to manipulate politics. This opens some space for the government to maneuver, including in relations with India: Nawaz Sharif can initiate a rapprochement with India provided it does not lead to the abandonment of any of Pakistan's traditional claims.

On the Indian side, Modi does not consider Pakistan a priority. India would benefit from better relations with Pakistan, but its economic future does not depend on it. Yet all previous attempts to ignore Pakistan ended up with the resumption of terrorist attacks, a situation that India wants to avoid, not least because a possible escalation into even a conventional conflict with Pakistan could impede the new government's program of economic reform.

Pakistan, although the weaker of the two actors, controls to a large extent the evolution of the relationship. But the choice facing Islamabad involves more than its bilateral relations with India. Pakistan must decide between joining the development bandwagon, or becoming increasingly marginalized in the international community. Making this decision will require that Pakistan speak with a single voice, including both the government and the security establishment. Given the configuration of Pakistan's polity, only a consolidation of democracy in the country will allow for substantial improvements in the relationship with India. But this will be, at best, an incremental process.

Bilateral relations are, therefore, likely to fluctuate between periods of appeasement and occasional crisis. There is little chance of a major conflict, but the worsening of the security situation on both countries' fringes in Afghanistan and Kashmir could revive the risk of terrorism, possibly in Predictability also applies to foreign policy. Observers in the United States blanch at the prospect of a Prime Minister Narendra Modi, the candidate of the right-wing Bharatiya Janata Party (BJP), whom they believe may apply his Hindutva, or Hindu nationalist, beliefs to Indian foreign policy. Their worry is shared by many Indians, who believe him to be at best indifferent to, and at worst hostile to, the concerns of Indian Muslims. What the effect of a Modi government would be on Indian domestic politics is an open question. But no matter who assumes the country's highest office, the broad contours of Indian foreign policy are not likely to change dramatically.

A look at Indian foreign policy since 1964 confirms that it has been characterized more by continuity than by change. And even those changes that have occurred, while important, have been incremental, and unrelated to the political ideology of the party in power. After all, as a serving Indian ambassador recently told me, "An elephant is not prone to making sharp turns."

For many years, much to the Indian government's annoyance, the country's relationship with Pakistan defined India on the world stage. Despite regime changes in New Delhi and Islamabad and numerous diplomatic initiatives, cease-fires, and bilateral talks, Kashmir's status is as unresolved today as it was 50 years ago, and relations continue to be overtly hostile, with the ever-present possibility of war. Although the conflict is often framed as one between Hindus and Muslims, a secular Congress Party–led government has been no more or less likely to be conciliatory toward Pakistan than a Hindu Nationalist BJP-led government. In fact, three major peace initiatives with Pakistan occurred under BJP prime minister Atal Bihari Vajpayee's watch: "bus diplomacy" in 1999, the Agra summit in 2001, and the Islamabad summit in 2004. Second, Pakistan's military, which remains the country's most powerful institution, continues to be uninterested in moving closer to India through channels other than trade and economics. It also bears mentioning that Pakistan's armed forces derive much of their legitimacy -- as well as their role in politics -- from an India that remains estranged from Pakistan. In effect, so long as there is no peace with India, Pakistan's military can argue that India poses an existential threat, thereby justifying the military's need to be active across the Pakistani state.

Third, there is a disconnect at play with regard to each country's desired agenda in future peace talks. Pakistan's government has viewed a formal trade relationship with India as a possible springboard for discussions on the bigger issues, such as territorial disputes like Kashmir. By contrast, India's government sees trade normalization as an end in itself. This latter position is rooted in New Delhi's view that Jammu and Kashmir are an inalienable and irrevocable part of India.

So is there any hope that Modi's grand gesture to Sharif back in May can trigger a new era in bilateral relations? In the short term, the answer is likely to be no. Historically, bilateral relations have resembled a boomerang: Efforts toward reconciliation have proceeded in fits and starts, with steps forward and hopes raised --followed by steps back and hopes dashed. Just when progress is being made, disaster strikes. In the 1950s, India was Pakistan's largest trade partner, but by 1965, the two countries were at war. In the short term, it will be difficult for the two countries to extricate themselves from this fits-and-starts pattern, and to find new sustained patterns of relating to one another.

As for the long term, hope for better bilateral relations lies in focusing on areas that have the potential to bring shared benefits to both countries, not only in commonly discussed areas such as trade and investment, but also in other areas such as energy or water resources. This is an objective that would need to be pursued through a renewed Composite Dialogue or quiet back-channel diplomacy.

In a blow to efforts to improve relations with Pakistan, India has cancelled talks scheduled for next week in Islamabad. The move comes after India's prime minister accused Pakistan of conducting a proxy war in Kashmir. until a few days ago the signs from New Delhi and Islamabad had been positive. Pakistan's Prime Minister Nawaz Sharif had been invited to New Delhi to attend Narendra Modi's inauguration as India's prime minister in May. Top level bilateral talks between the two foreign secretaries were scheduled to take place in Islamabad next week. Both sides had refrained from indulging in the usual diplomatic blame games and had toned down the rhetoric considerably in recent months. All of this had given rise to considerable hopes that the two countries could possibly find a way to restart the so-called composite dialogue India had suspended after the 2008 terrorist attacks in Mumbai allegedly carried out by the Lahore-based Islamist Lashkar-e-Taiba organisation.

But these hopes have been dashed for the time being with India's decision to cancel Foreign Secretary Sujata Singh's visit to the capital of Pakistan next week. To an outsider the reason for the cancellation of the talks appears plausible. India has said that the decision of Pakistan's High Commissioner to India, Abdul Basit, to hold talks with separatists from the part of Kashmir that is under Indian administration "raises questions about Pakistan's sincerity and undermines the constructive diplomatic efforts by India's new prime minister." But in view of the fact that Pakistan has previously spoken to militants from Kashmir without facing a backlash of this severity from India, there is clearly more to this than meets the eye.

So what has triggered this about turn by the Indian government? After cross-border skirmishes across the line of control in Kashmir in the last few days, Modi has been put on the spot. The hardline Hindu-nationalist leader cannot afford to appear weak in the eyes of his domestic constituency as he pledged to strengthen India during the election. Kashmir has been at the centre of a territorial dispute between the two countries since independence in 1947. The nuclear-armed neighbors have fought three wars in sixty-seven years and nearly went to war as recently as 2008 after the Mumbai attacks. Without a doubt, India feels that Islamist terrorists are again trying to foment trouble in Kashmir and that they have been given a green light to do so from their paymasters in Islamabad. This assessment was clearly behind Modi's remarks last week before he visited Kashmir when he accused Pakistan of waging a proxy war in the region.

For Pakistan's Prime Minister Nawaz Sharif, the cancellation of the talks is nothing short of a disaster. By travelling to New Delhi to Modi's inauguration he put his prestige on the line. In the process he took the risk of challenging the powerful industrial-military complex at home run by the armed forces and their omnipresent intelligence service ISI. The very legitimation for their ubiquitous influence on Pakistani foreign and security policy depends upon the maintenance of significant tension with India. Without a perceived threat from their powerful neighbors, ordinary Pakistanis would not accept the inordinate size of the military budget or the fact that ISI operates without supervision by the Pakistani government.

Nawaz Sharif himself clearly has expressed a strong interest in improving trading ties with India and relaxing political tensions. He hopes that this will be of mutual benefit and help him lead his country out of its desperate financial and economic situation. He is the last person in Islamabad who would have given a green light for a resurgence of Islamist terrorism in Kashmir.

It is however well documented that the Pakistani intelligence service, ISI, has trained and financed Islamist terrorists in the past with the aim of destabilizing Indian Kashmir. The timing of the recent cross-border incursions and attacks by Islamists is no coincidence. It serves as a provocation to Hindu strongman Modi and guarantees humiliation for the

Pakistani Prime Minister, who at present has his hands full at home in the face of massive anti-government demonstrations organized by opposition politician Imran Khan and Muslim cleric Tahirul Qadri. Both of these men are suspected of having close links to the military establishment in Pakistan.

Thus it would appear that the opponents of a rapprochement between India and Pakistan have won the opening political battle in the Modi-Sharif era. It is a powerful warning to Sharif to abandon his policies. But the fact remains that both men need each other to address their pressing economic problems. The question now is whether they can overcome the opposition at home. The outlook is bleak.

Relations between India and its historic rival Pakistan have deteriorated sharply in recent weeks, especially after India's government, now led by the Hindu supremacist Bharatiya Janata Party (BJP), cancelled a much anticipated meeting between the countries' Foreign Secretaries.

Two "flag meetings" between locally-based Indian and Pakistani military officers were held at LoC checkpoints last week, the second of them on Friday. These meetings have done little to dampen tensions, as the two sides focused on trading accusations of responsibility for the surge in cross-border firing and incursions. uch meetings, however, have long been accepted and even facilitated by India's government, including under the BJP-led governments that held power in New Delhi from 1998 to 2004.

That India's actions constitute an attempt to rewrite the "ground rules" for Indian-Pakistan relations is openly conceded by the Indian media and by government officials in off-the-record remarks. "That there is a discontinuity in India's approach is exactly right," observed C. Raja Mohan, an Indian foreign policy expert, in his Indian Express column. "The Modi government is now saying there is no place for the Hurriyat in the peace process with Pakistan. Delhi's new approach is a bold gamble, to say the least."

1

India Pakistan Relations: A Brief Sketch

India Pakistan relations are now bound to change due to the change of international contours of the world. The US is no more interested in cajoling Pakistan as a soft Islamic state nor is China whole heartedly keen to frog lift Pakistan. On the other hand a strong leadership in India has flagged of a strong message to create a cohesive South Asian structures with willingness of almost all the concerned countries of South Asia. If this rail moves on track Pakistan may be left out in the race in South Asia. That is how India Pakistan Relations has moved to a different level.

One question that has often been asked of Pakistanis in the recent months is what do we think about Modi as a prime minister? My counter question is do we as neighbors get to choose who is elected to office in New Delhi or elsewhere? No; but what we can do is aim towards setting realistic goals instead of drawing rosy pictures or trying to thread the string from where the last Bharatiya Janata Government (BJP) government left it at: the Lahore Declaration or the much talked about Chenab river plan. Narendra Modi is not Atal Behari Vajpayee, and despite being elected from the platform and being Kar Sevaks of the Rashtriya Swayamsevak Sangh (RSS), the two could not be more different. They have very different visions and orientations, and are set almost a generation apart. In very realistic terms, we should not expect Modi to act like his predecessor, as Vajpayee had a vision, which was baptised by the hardcore realities that he himself was a participatory to, and wanted to leave a legacy of peace between the two neighbors despite stiff opposition from his party cadres and policy makers. Much has changed over the last decade, with more interest groups favoring the constituency of conflict than peace. At best, what Pakistan would see is some positive movement on the economic front. At the micro level, this would prove beneficial and may indirectly strengthen the somewhat vocal trade and commerce constituency that has constantly pressed for enhanced bilateral trade. In fact, in December 2011, Modi, as the Chief Minister of Gujarat, was invited by a visiting delegation of the Karachi Chamber of Commerce and Industry to visit the city and showcase the successful "Gujarat Model." But the trip did not materialise for various reasons – one amongst them being, Modi's alleged role in the 2002 riots where several Muslims were killed. If the two prime ministers come together on the economic front, there would be enhanced bilateral trade, and increased Afghan transit trade as well. The second benefit could be increased cooperation in the energy sector, as speculations point towards a potential 500 MW electricity transmission line from India to Pakistan – that would bring some respite to the energy-stressed country. However, on the economic front, Pakistan also needs to keep in mind that changing regional dynamics entail shifting politico-economic priorities, and with Modi being touted as South Asian Shinzo Abe, all the world powers would be keen to pursue better commercial relations with New Delhi.

Regretably, however, positive development towards resolving key contentious issues is unlikely. Those issues will remain stalemated, and when bilateral talks will finally be scheduled and rebooted, the pattern would be the same: talks for the sake of continuing with talks. However, the more concerning notion is the possibility of New Delhi revoking Article 370 of the Indian Constitution, which accords special status to the Indian-held Jammu and Kashmir. Not only would such an action hold drastic consequences for the occupied valley and its relations with New Delhi, but across the Line of Control, it could trigger a similar move, creating a political compulsion for Pakistan to react in a similar fashion. In Pakistan, Kashmir's final legal status lay pending under Article 257 of the Pakistani Constitution. Although it would not be very easy to repeal Article 370, most of its provisions have already been violated over the years. Lastly and most dangerously, it will also give credence to right wing elements to oppose any bilateral ties, promote armed agitation and violence by militants and indigenous Kashmiri resistance groups.

Relations among nations are the natural outcome of co-existence. Its nature is determined by the internal compulsions of nations and external forces which are at play. Foreign policy's importance can be analyzed in the light of the fact that it is the only policy that proposes interaction among nations. Relations between two countries represent policies of two countries. These policies have direct implications of foreign policy of nation states which decided the course of international politics.

Nations does not exist in vacuum, they exist in a particular environment and have to adopt it, like any other organism. Consequently any change in the environment requires change in the behavior of the nations. No nation is nor can be fully self-sufficient, for the ends that it wishes to achieve always outweigh the resources that it has. Infect the desire to fulfill the national interest and the inability to achieve all the goals of foreign policy independently gives rise to the configuration called interdependence of nations. Interdependence is an incontrovertible fact of international relations and this precisely is the reason why every nations gets involved in the process of establishing bilateral and multilateral relations leading to diplomatic political, economic, cultural and trade relations with other nations. A nation not only has to respond to the new changes but also has to achieve its foreign policy goals by skillful handling of the global milieu. . "A nation follows a policy that is most beneficial to its own national interest, which largely depends on ideology, history and economic requirements".

The making of foreign policy depends on various issues such as external threat, geographical location, strategic significance political aspirations, economic requirements, ideology, and personality of the statesmen and over all national interests. The root of tension between the two neighbours lies in their history and a psychology of negativism and bitterness which has developed over the years due to the non resolution of tensions and their exploitation by the ruling elite in their own interest.

India and Pakistan are the core states of South Asia which are culturally similar linguistically unite geographically closed and historically related. But it is strange that despite the geographical, historical and cultural similarity the relations between these two states not so much smooth and peaceful. The demand for Pakistan was itself based on distrust. Roots of this kind of relationship between India-Pakistan can be seen in the colonial history of Indian subcontinent. British colonial rules established a tradition by the partition of this subcontinent that creates a chain of struggles, disputes and instability in the region. Bilateral relations between India and Pakistan are undoubtedly the most important in South Asia and the world also. But relations among both states not at all smooth in nature and has been full of ups and downs. Now the both countries are overtly nuclear powered, they poses greater risk, if the ongoing crisis is not resolved. It is in this background, the study of Indo-Pak relations is an attempt to analyze the Political, Economic, Strategic issues and other related bilateral issues between these two countries. And efforts will be made to suggest methods by which the peace and security can be maintain in the region. The relation between India and Pakistan can be categorized since 1947 in five different phases. These phases are (a) Process of partition and separation (1947-1954), (b) period of Conflicting relations (1955-1971), (c) Period of efforts to make peace and good relationship (1972-1979), (d) Period of ups and downs (1980-1998), and (e) The period of new beginning (since 1999 to till now). This study is related to the last phase which started since 1998 when both countries conducted nuclear tests in May, 1998. India conducted her five nuclear tests in Pokharn and Pakistan conducted her six nuclear tests in Chhagai. After these tests the relations between India and Pakistan is changed. Both nations start thinking to establish peace and cooperation in the region. After May, 1998 both nations started conversation and tried to find way to CBMs between themselves. The changed environment of this region shows the new beginning of Indo-Pak relationship.

Historical Background:

The history of Indo-Pak Relations has been mainly a story of conflict and discord, mutual distrust and suspicion. Other than Israel, Pakistan is the only nation in 20th century whose birth resulted from the demand by a religious community for a political structure in which it would be dominant. In the August, 1947 British India was divided into two parts as decolonization process that was the birth of the two independent nations in the subcontinent namely India and Pakistan. Since, India and Pakistan, became independent it has been rightly stated that Pakistan's foreign policy is made in India but unfortunately India and Pakistan never became good friends and always engaged in conflicts and disputes. There is a fair amount of scholarly agreement that partition occurred not because of Hindus and Muslim could not live together, but because the elite of the two communities could not agree to power sharing. The greatest tragedy was that the deciding feature of this division was religion. These two nations never come out from the circle of conflicts and disputes since independence. Their relations travel from dispute to peace and peace to dispute subsequently but remain always far from friendship and cooperation. It has resulted from a number of complex factors like legacy, the difference in religion and race, conflicting national interests, ideologies, power struggle. From the very beginning, the two powers became involved in a conflict ridden relationship over the status of the former princely state of Jammu and Kashmir and forced immigrate of thousands of Hindu and Muslim into the new countries which affected both emerging countries. The dispute has proved severely opposed to resolution because, at bottom, it is infused with the self-images of the two states. Pakistan deemed its identity as a Muslim homeland incomplete without Kashmir; while India sees its control over this Muslim-majority state as a demonstration of its secular identification. This tense relationship has resulted in three major wars (1947-48, 1965, 1971) and a limited one (1999) and multiple crises like the question of minorities, evacuee property, sharing of assert, divison of military stores, Hadrabad and Junagarh --- the list is endless. A number of promising agreements were made were made. For instance, the Tashkent and Shimla agreements, and Lahor declaration. Although they resolved the Indus Waters dispute in 1960 and the Rann of Kutch dispute in 1968 through negotiations, there was no agreed mechanism to guide their stable conflictual relationship. After 1971, consequent the liberation of East Pakistan and formation of Bangladesh, India gained legitimate status of being an emerging power in South Asia. In the 1980s the two sides began to talk on the Siachen, Sir Creek and the Tulbul-Wullar disputes and put in place a series of confidence building measures pertaining to conventional and nuclear weapons power. These negotiations had no set time table and were held on a need to meet basis. There was no compulsion on either side to continue their negotiations when their relationship declined in the face of terrorist attack or armed aggression.

However, with the coming in of the BJP government in 1998, and the nuclear tests by both states give status of nuclear power to these. The period between 1999 and 2002 witnessed a high level of tension between India and Pakistan. Indian Prime Minister Vajpai started a bus service between Delhi and Lahore on 20 Feb, 1999 by a great journey through this bus. At the time of this journey the Prime Minister signed a MOU (Memorandums of Understanding) with their Pakistani counterpart on 21 Feb, 1999. This MOU known as the Lahore declaration. In this declaration the focused was given on co-operations, to fight against terrorism, to give respect to human rights, to don't interfere in their internal issues and to behave like good neighbors. But unfortunately Pakistan started war against India in May, 1999 in the Kargil but this become a great tensions between these nations. After Kargil conflict and attacks on J&K legislative assembly and Indian Parliament in 2001 there was tensions on border across LOC and the ceasefire declared. The Prime Minister of India Atal Bihari Vajpayee extending "the hand of friendship" towards Pakistan. Pakistan responded large number of CBMs including announcement of the ceasefire on the LOC. Thus there is many ups and downs between these nations in the last century.

The peace process launched in January 2004 had been one of the most productive and sustained in the history of a dismal bilateral relationship. This process has seen significant expansion of bilateral trade, improved people to people contact, a ceasefire on their borders, the implementation of number of confidence-building measures in disputed Kashmir, and above all serious back channel negotiation on the Kashmir question. While its policy makers have increasingly talked about the urgent need to construct a 'peaceful periphery' for many of its leader an integrated north west region of the subcontinent was a living memory. None exemplifies this better than Prime Minister Man Mohan Singh of India, who's family lived in the north west part of what is now Pakistan and migrated to India after partition. In early 2007, speaking on India's relations with its neighbors, Singh mused on his aspirations for restoring these historic connections:

"I sincerely believe... that the destiny of the people of South Asia is interlinked. It is not just our past that links us, but our future too. India cannot be a prosperous, dynamic economy and a stable polity if our neighborhood as a whole is also not economically prosperous and politically stable. Similarly, our neighbors cannot prosper if India does not do so as well. There are enormous opportunities for promoting mutually beneficial cooperation in South Asia. To exploit these opportunities, the nations of South Asia have to work sincerely to control the scourge of terrorism and extremism... I dream of a day, while retaining our respective national identities, one can have breakfast in Amritsar, lunch in Lahore and dinner in Kabul. That is how my forefathers lived. That is how I want to our grandchildren to live."

Today, more than sixty five years after independence, the common people as well as the elite of India and Pakistan are concerning towards establishing condition for permanent peace. But unfortunately the situation is not so much better for India and Pakistan which it should be but the power of the old mindset is declining and the momentum for peace is growing.

Relevance of the Study:

It is well documented that in contrast to India, Pakistan started its journey as an independent state without the political infrastructure around which democracy could grow and develop. This institutional deficit created the space for the early rise of the military as an autonomous and powerful actor in domestic politics in Pakistan but in India, civil authority is supreme. Therefore if democracy succeeds in Pakistan then peaceful environment can be harvested in South Asia. India is very much alive to this and has made considerable efforts in this direction and wanting a stable neighbour at peace with itself. Yet, the Indian Strategy has not been able to translate the intent into reality. There is no doubt that people on both sides want contact, not distance. In 2006, the year of writing, it had to be seen to be believed. A huge number of people gathered at the same border nearly 500,000 people had only one slogan on their lips: 'Hindustan Pakistan dosti zindabad' (long live India-Pakistan friendship') . This shows that people of both states want always live together, then why government of both states cannot engage for permanent peace of the subcontinent. In this row foreign secretary Nirupama Rao and her Pakistani counterpart Salman Bashir in Thimphu on the sidelines of a South Asian Association for Regional Cooperation(SAARC,2010) meeting and agreed to hold talks on traditional issues as well as talks incorporating a new subject Afghanistan and came up with new ideas and said that "why should we be just struck with discussing these issues, why cannot we discuss more issues? Why cannot we discuss the situation in our region?" Further Indian foreign Minister S M Krishna and his Pakistani counterpart Hina Rabbani Khar announced new Confidence Building Measures (CBMs) and expected that these will expand the scope of people to people contacts and humanitarian issues. The CBMs include increasing cross-LOC trading days and expanding travel to include tourism and religious aspects, apart from relaxing permit conditions for travel by people of Jammu and Kashmir to the other side of LOC by having a system of Six month multiple entry.

Both countries had tried everything including war and mobilization of troops to force the other to accept its version of Kashmir Settlement. They failed in this. Secondly, nuclear parity in South Asia made war almost impossible. Thirdly, the economies of both the countries were doing very well at this time and the rising middle classes in both countries desired peace for continued growth. Pakistan has at realized that it will be a gained by according the most favored nation status to India in matters of trade and commerce. India took such a decision in the case of Pakistan a few years back. Pakistan's community has made a strong recommendation for MFN status to India, saying that it changed scenario. This necessitated an alternative strategy for a solution of the Kashmir dispute which would satisfy the people of Kashmir, India, Pakistan. That being the case, it was clear that any solution we found would not be an ideal one from the perspective of all Kashmiri's, Pakistani's, and Indians. It could only be the best under the circumstances.

Despite all this it was convinced that we were on the wrong track as far as neighborhood management was concerned. We needed a new approach to convert the traditional confrontation and conflict approach to one of cooperation and convergence. People in South Asia, home to a vast majority of the world's poor, need the availability of employment opportunities more than anything else. This is essential so that no one takes interest in destructive activities like terrorism. If there is cooperation between India and Pakistan and not conflict, vast opportunities will open up for trade, travel and development that will create prosperity in both nations.

Third Party Factor:

Bilateralism in Indo-Pak relations remains the fundamental principle of conflict resolution initiatives. The 1972 Simla agreement signed following the 1971 war provided that both parties will settle their pending disputes through bilateral negotiations or through any other means mutually agreed upon between them. This agreement ruled out the possibility of any third party involvement in Indo-Pakistan affairs, especially on the disputes which are being negotiated within the rubric of the eight baskets mechanism. But here is not to deny the influence of the third party indirect influence, particularly the United States, in Indo-Pak relations. In the 1990s, after the withdrawal of the Soviet troops in Afghanistan, there was a discernible plunge in US interest in Pakistan on the one hand and growing warmth in relations with India on the other. Such a paradigm shift in US foreign policy added to Pakistan's insecurity, driving it to establish a mechanism for engagement with India to address its security interests, independent of US support. The need for Pakistan to engage India in dialogue continues today. Likewise, the rapprochement with China with both sides bolstering their trade relations and engaging in talks to resolve their boundary disputes indicated India's increasing control over its foreign relations with neighbours, who also had good relations with Pakistan. As a result Pakistan was slowly coming to terms with the new realities in which, like India and China, it needed to move away from a confrontationist approach towards a policy of engagement and address pending disputes in a peaceful and negotiated manner. The conventional wisdom that one cannot chose neighbours and therefore must learn to live with them had begun to shape India and Pakistan's foreign policy formulations, irrespective of the challenges and difficulties such an approach entailed.

Theoretical Perspective:

Since the independence and partition of India and Pakistan in 1947 the relationship between these two states has been the most intractable and the most dangerous political standoff in South Asia. Since the end of the cold war it is perhaps the most dangerous and unpredictable region in international politics. There are several reasons for this continuing tension like the hostility between the Indian National Congress (INC) and the Muslim League prior to independence, hostility that carried over into the post 1947 period, the bloodletting that occurred at partition, served even further to entrench hostility between them leading both to question the justification and legitimacy of each other and within weeks of independence Kashmir became and remains a continued source of political, ideological and military friction between them. Barry Buzan suggests, "their historical, geographic and cultural ties do not allow them to ignore each other...but their organization principles pose a permanent threat to each other." India and Pakistan were founded on two very different ideological foundations. India constituted a secular state, whereby religion would play no part in the body politic. Pakistan founded as a Muslim state, a home for the Muslims of South Asia. The crux of these antagonisms has manifested itself in a conflict of self and other with both states questioning the legitimacy of the other. This complex relationship should be subject to a method of theorization that seeks a greater understanding of the nature or culture of violence between them. Such an approach has been lacking in accounts of relations in South Asia.

This section will begin with a brief outline of where the theoretical approach being used here fits into the international relations theory literature. This is important because IR struggles to account for Indo-Pakistan relations due to the unique structural and ideational position of these two states after 1947. India and Pakistan born out of the same struggle for independence share these contradictions between the very old and the very new. Very old given the ancient civilization from where they came and very new given that they both entered the international system as sovereign states, a system that was unfamiliar to the experience of both. Maya Chadda points to the difficulties IR theory has in grappling with this problem when she suggests it might be more useful to imagine South Asia not as a region or subcontinent of separate sovereign states, "but as one of graded ethnic differences." This too brings us back to bridging the gap between primordial's arguments of ethnic kin set against the modern theatre of nation states and realist debates about states being unitary actors and the balance of power.

Stephen Cohen brings this problem into sharp relief by what he terms the, 'realism-idealism conundrum.' This description gives a good insight into the India Pakistan relations poses for international relations theorists due to its uncomfortable sovereign structure in 1947. The answer to these problematic theoretical and policy issues is found in Alexander Wendt's constructivist approach because it has elements of foundationalism and also contains a degree of relativism. Moreover, Wendt occasionally refers to his theoretical approach as 'structural ideation' which again shows the attempt at establishing a via media between positivist structure and post positivist ideation. If we are to get to grips with the methodological and theoretical problems that India - Pakistan relations presents then a method whereby a structural idealism approach can be developed and deployed is essential. Moreover constructivism contends that individuals and states act differently towards objects, including other actors, on the basis of the meaning they attach to them. It is to say that actors react differently to objects or other actors in a manner that is preordained by meaning, not materialism. Wendt writes, "US military power has a different meaning for Canada than for Cuba, despite their 'structural' positions, just as British missiles have a different significance for the United States than do Soviet missiles. The distribution of power may always affect states' calculations, but how it does so depends on the, inter subjective understandings and expectations on the distribution of knowledge, that constitute their conceptions of Self and Other." If Wendt is right and power politics is socially constructed by a process of inter-subjective modes of behavior, then India Pakistan relations is replete with examples. Not least the sectarianism born out of partition, both states claim to be nuclear weapon states and both have prosecuted war against one another since 1947. Indian missiles do not threaten Sri Lanka and Pakistani missiles do not threaten the security of Nepal. Therefore it can be argued that there are other reductionist dynamics at work. Anarchy is not a given as structural realists argue, at a reductionist level, inter subjective knowledge is playing a causal role in informing what meaning states attach to the other states military capability. This for constructivism is not a structural or material dynamic purely about power politics, but a dynamic that is informed by knowledge and informed by the way states take each other into account.

Power politics then is, 'produced causally by processes of interaction between states in which anarchy plays only a permissive role.' Within this theoretical remit the power of the structural realist suggestion that wars occurs because there is nothing to prevent it becomes less persuasive and is demoted as a causal mechanism to one of, war occurs because war occurs. Or perhaps, war occurs because states let them occur. The systemic explanation as to the cause of war moves away from a systemic anarchy towards a more state identity or reductionist explanation that allows states to interact between each other as opposed to being given a purely reactionary role within the self-help system. Constructivism argues therefore that states act differently toward enemies than they do toward friends because enemies are threatening and friends are not. 'Anarchy and the distribution of power are insufficient to tell us which. US military power has a different significance for Canada than for Cuba, despite their similar 'structural' position.' Wendt conceptualizes this role of anarchy in its rump form as an empty vessel that has no intrinsic logic or specific form and that anarchies only acquire logics as a function of what states put inside them. In parlance with the empty vessel metaphor, the international structure is the empty vessel and interests and identity need to be given greater theoretical power in accounting for the nature of anarchies because what states put into the vessel, in terms of ideas of culture and interests, is international politics.

Cultures of Anarchy

The two cultures of anarchy are adopted from two different philosophical and theoretical approaches that reflect the different understandings as to the state of nature and the subsequent role of the state and the structural debates about what the role of the state is and to what extent the behavior of states is determined. In Hobbesian culture it is 'enemy' and in a Lockean culture it is 'rival.' Both involve a different posture or orientation of the self and other with respect to the use of violence and levels of violence.

The posture of a Hobbesian 'enemy' culture is one of survival where the use of violence has no limitation. In a Lockean 'rival' culture the use of violence is considered for the purpose of advancing an interest or to secure a specific objective. These two cultures of anarchy will be outlined below and it will be suggested that the two levels or cultures are needed to take into account the unique structure or contours of the relationship which after 1947 has shown signs of both Hobbesian and Lockean cultures of anarchy. The culture of anarchy between India and Pakistan is one where ideas and identity prevail over structure. It has not only been Kashmir it has been Bangladesh, Punjab, or Baluchistan, knowledge is partial and amorphous and has always prevailed over structure.

In a Hobbesian culture of anarchy survival is the key and the amount of violence one is prepared to inflict on the other reflects a kill or be killed attitude. Enemies are representations of the other as an actor who,[1] does not recognize the right of the self to exist as an actor to exist as an autonomous being and therefore[2] will not willingly limit its violence toward the self. It is the emphasis on survival that gives the Hobbesian culture its hard edge and why it is the most extreme and dangerous of the two anarchies. This limitless recourse to violence is explained by the fundamental of survival, it moves beyond conflict whereby violence might be gauged to meet a limited objective into a sphere where an enemy does not recognize the right of the other to exist. This is the Hobbesian view of the state of nature, or where the use of violence is limited only by material exhaustion.

Treating the other in terms of a Hobbesian enemy has several implications for a state's foreign policy posture and the history of India Pakistan relations is replete with examples. First, a state being treated as other in the Hobbesian sense will try to respond in kind or by pre-emption and in so doing, move away from what might have been a status quo position to being forced into a kill or be killed mode. Second, the decision making process moves to a worst case scenario where the possibilities rather than probabilities will dominate the process, thus negating any chance of rapprochement and relegating the chances of a third party successfully intervening to prevent further escalation. Third, and critically in the case of India and Pakistan, relative military capabilities become crucial and become the benchmark used to predict the behavior of an enemy. In other words, under a Hobbesian anarchy, military capability becomes the mechanism used to predict the behavior of an adversary because the other has already been established and is known as the enemy. Thus any political process has been usurped by military and relative military power of the enemy is used to predict the behavior of that enemy.

Moreover, once a Hobbesian anarchy is created (or socially constructed) states will behave in a manner that makes them an existential threat to the other. That is to say that it is the social construction between states that is resistant to change, far more than the system itself and that states which construct others as the enemy through shared ideas will be far more resistant to change. All sovereign states invent their traditions and history but given the political and cultural proximity of India and Pakistan prior to 1947 these two states have been forced to invent their traditions more than most other states in international politics. This has been a problem for security in the region given that one state identifies itself as being what the other is not.

The Lockean culture moves away from the kill or be killed Hobbesian emphasis of survival, to one of protection. The concept of rival has a very different meaning to both self and other and suggests the element of competition where violence is used in limited measure to secure an objective. Under a Lockean anarchy, states live within a status quo remit of live and let live whilst recognising the intrinsic right of other states to so the same. Sovereignty becomes a property, but becomes a right, only when other states recognize it as such and here is a key difference between the Hobbesian culture with its emphasis on survival and a Lockean culture which resides in the social recognition of sovereignty of one state to another. The units do not live in an international system of self-help and the units against the system, but share a greater amount of unit construction, the recognition of sovereignty being an important normative construct of states relations with each other. Thus sovereignty of the self allows for the recognition of the sovereign right of the other and this sustains the status quo position.

Despite the absence of a centralized authority or Leviathan most states adhere to this Lockean anarchy most of the time despite the major inequalities of material power and inequalities of economic and military capability. The Lockean system negates the realist imperative on the maximization of power because the 'rump materialism' of anarchy is controlled by the self, recognizing the sovereign right and legitimacy of the other. States by viewing each other as rivals, as opposed to enemies expect others to use limited violence to achieve a political objective but limit the use of violence to a limited set objective. An example of the use of limited violence is the 1982 Falklands conflict between Britain and Argentina where violence was limited to the sovereign ownership of the Islands. At no time during the conflict did Britain or Argentina question the right of the other to exist as sovereign entities. This is the key difference between an unlimited Hobbesian conflict of kill or be killed and a Lockean conflict limited to a specific objective, in this case the sovereign ownership of the Falkland Islands.

There are several implications coming out of the Lockean culture of anarchy for India Pakistan relations. The first is that this anarchy changes the meaning of military force and capability of the other. Whereas in a Hobbesian anarchy the rump materialism effect abounds, forcing states into a kill or be killed mode, under a Lockean anarchy there is more room for manoeuvre because the meaning of military power changes. In other words it is the type of anarchy states live under that gives meaning to military capability, thus the risk-aversion that states face with regard to their security, the threshold of risk is greatly reduced because states have more options given that they are not preoccupied with survival as under a Hobbesian culture. When states accept and internalize the Lockean system, recognition of sovereignty of the other greatly reduces the explanatory power of international anarchy and the self-help system because the system itself becomes less important than the recognition of the others sovereignty. Thus survival via recognition as opposed to the survival of the fittest becomes the norm in state relations and therefore it becomes in the interest of the self to recognise the other.

Relations between India and its historic rival Pakistan have deteriorated sharply in recent weeks. Last month saw a dramatic rise in cross-border firing along the Line of Control (LoC) that separates the Indian- and Pakistani-held sections of the former princely state of Jammu and Kashmir. The cross-border shelling has resulted in at least a half-dozen deaths and terrorized villagers on both sides of the LoC. By the beginning of last week, Indian government and military officials were issuing a barrage of threats against Pakistan. On a trip to Kashmir, Amit Shah, the BJP President and a close confidant of Indian Prime Minister Narendra Modi, pledged that India would give Pakistan a "befitting reply" if all cross-border firing did not cease.

Two "flag meetings" between locally-based Indian and Pakistani military officers were held at LoC checkpoints last week, the second of them on Friday. These meetings have done little to dampen tensions, as the two sides focused on trading accusations of responsibility for the surge in cross-border firing and incursions.Speaking Saturday, Indian Defence Minister Arun Jaitley said Pakistani violations of a 2003 ceasefire agreement were "extremely serious and provocative." On August 18, the Indian government announced that it was canceling the Foreign Secretaries' meeting planned for the following week. This was justified on the grounds that a meeting between the Pakistani High Commissioner to India, Abdul Basit, and leaders of the All Party Hurriyat Conference (APHC), an alliance of legally-tolerated Indian Kashmir separatist groups, constituted "gross interference" in Indian affairs Such meetings, however, have long been accepted and even facilitated by India's government, including under the BJP-led governments that held power in New Delhi from 1998 to 2004.

That India's actions constitute an attempt to rewrite the "ground rules" for Indian-Pakistan relations is openly conceded by the Indian media and by government officials in off-the-record remarks.

"That there is a discontinuity in India's approach is exactly right," observed C. Raja Mohan, an Indian foreign policy expert, in his Indian Express column. "The Modi government is now saying there is no place for the Hurriyat in the peace process with Pakistan. Delhi's new approach is a bold gamble, to say the least."

A senior government official told MailOnlineIndia that the decision to cancel the Foreign Secretaries' meeting had been "made at the highest level" and was aimed at establishing "new ground rules" for India's relations with Pakistan. With a Modi-led BJP-government in power in New Delhi, it would not be "business as usual" between the two nuclear-armed states, said the official.

Footnote

1. Poonam Mann, Indias Foreign Policy in the Post Cold War era, Harman Publishing House, New Delhi, 2000, P. 1.
2. R.S.Yadav, and Suresh Dhanda (eds.) Indias Foreign Policy, Contemporary Trends, Shipra, Delhi, 2009, p. 1.
3. Kapil Kak, " Pakistan: A Geo-Political Appriaisal", Strategic Analysis, vol.22, n.8, November 1998, p. 1124.
4. Rajesh Rajagopalan, " Neorealist Theory and the India-Pakistan Conflicet*-I", Strategic Analysis, vol.22, n.9, December 1998, p. 1269.
5. Jugal Kishore Misra, "Indo-Pak Relations: A Relook", World Focus, Vol.33, no.11, November,2012, p.62.
6. The Times of India, February 17, 2011.
7. Ali Ahmed, "India-Pakistan Relations: Military Diplomacy Vs Strategic Engagement", Journal of Defence Studies and Analyses, vol.5, no.1, January,2011.
8. Kuldip Nayar "People to People Contact" op. cit, no.4, pp.88-89.

2

Political Factors of India Pakistan Conflict

The political structures of the two countries are in contrast. Indian structures over period of time gradually matured its political institutions whereas Pakistan remained lost in identifying its real cause of existence. This gaffe has been filled by the fundamentalist forces. The name sake of democracy failed to deliver. The terrorist outfits seeped into the power gallery and started making important decisions. This chapter looks into the lens of political factors and different structures in Pakistan.

The root causes of India-Pakistan rift can be traced back to the days before the division of the subcontinent. Until the arrival of Muslim traders, missionaries, and armies in the late seventh and early eighth centuries, the population of South Asia was primarily Hindu and Buddhist. By A.D. 1100 a number of Indo-Muslim states had been established and by the sixteenth century the Mughal Empire dominated northern India. The British formally disbanded the empire in 1858, at which time about one quarter of India's population were Muslims. They were concentrated in East Bengal, the Northwest Frontier, Punjab, Sindh, and Blauchistan, with large Muslim minorities in present day Uttar Pradesh and Madhya Pradesh. Indian Muslim slowly adapted to British rule yet maintained their identity, establishing the Aligarh Muslim University (1875) and the Muslim League (1906). The latter, dominated by wealthy landowners and Muslim professionals, was largely secular in orientation; through a basic concern was the fate of Muslim in mainly Hindu political order. There was no suggestion of a separate Muslim state until 1930, when the Punjabi poet-politician Mohammed Iqbal raised the idea. Three year later a group of Indian students at Cambridge proposed naming it Pakistan. As the prospects of British withdrawal from South Asia increased, the Muslim League, led by the lawyer- politician Mohammed Ali Jinnah, declared its support for the idea of Pakistan in its historic address in 1940 Lahore session that set forth the logic of Pakistan.[1]

The Hindus and the Muslim belong to two different religious philosophies, social customs, and literatures. They neither inter-marry, nor inter-dine together and indeed, they belong to two different civilizations which are based mainly on conflicting ideas and conceptions. Their aspects on life are different. It is quite clear that Hindus and Musalmans derive their inspiration from different sources of history. They have different epics, their heroes are different, and they have different episodes. Very often the hero of one is a foe of the other, and likewise, their victories and defeats overlap.

Jinnah turned the "two-nation" theory into an effective political movement by trying to weld together disparate elements of the Indian Muslim community. Another reason behind the partition, a separate status for India's Muslim was became an important milestone on the road leading to Pakistan. Despite the increasing support for Pakistan—whether as a separate entity within India or as a state—many distinguished Indian Muslims rejected the idea, choosing to be loyal to the politically dominant Indian National Congress. What percentage of Indian Muslims favored an independent Pakistan is still unclear, but there is no doubt that the most prominent community leaders wanted a separate state—or at least staked out a claim for Pakistan in the hope of winning concessions in the final round of negotiations. The third towering figure of this group was Allama Iqbal, who in his own way propelled the idea of Pakistan forward as effectively as Jinnah or Sir Syed.[2]

Pakistan has been on the roller-coaster of democracy and dictatorship and a war against India always meant a change in Pakistan. An adventure against India is necessarily the outcome of compelling domestic circumstances. Therefore, Pakistan has always been conscious of its leadership role in Islamic world. This goes much beyond the two nation theory, which fulfilled itself with the partition of India (1947).[3] On the eve of partition both parties created images of each other which continued to be major elements of the entire conflict. The Indian National Congress maintained that old India continued to exist as an entity, though the secession of some areas was agreed to in the conviction that what remained would be integrated into a strong unified state. On its part the Muslim League stressed that the Muslim majority areas in the northwest and east India constituted into a separate state, would grow into a strong, strategically vital Muslim state. There are two major reasons for the persistence of this kind of conflict, the antithetical nature of Hinduism and Islam, and the other, consequences of

Britain's 'cut and run' departure from the subcontinent. Besides the conflict between the competing visions of Islam and secularism, sharp differences could be found in the history and policies of the two major political parties, The Muslim League and The Indian National Congress. To begin with, the issue of separate electorates demanded by The Muslim League was vehemently opposed by the Congress. This type of environment leads the subcontinent towards partition.

Thus, since 1947 both states have enduring divergences over a number of issues in which their perceptions and images have played a decisive role in shaping their overall policies.[4] Formal partition was only the beginning that implemented on 14 August, 1947, the actual separation between the people of India and Pakistan was a slow process spreads over several decades. Few people in India and Pakistan care to remember that things were very different in the early years. Initially there were no passports or identity papers, and no visas. People could easily travel to the other side of the new border; some lived in one country and worked in the other. There were regular train and ferry services in India and Pakistan. Films from one country were freely shown in the other, and film songs were aired by national radio stations without regards to nationality. Cultural exchange like Urdu mushairas (poetry recitals) were quit common because Urdu was still a thriving language in the northern and other parts of India, and was held by Pakistanis as there national language. Indian publications were freely available in Pakistani markets, and vice versa. For a while even Pakistan's currency was printed in India. Until the late 1950s, Pakistani Universities benefited from Indian professors by inviting them to examine students in Pakistan. Some Indian professors would take a night train to Lahore conduct the examination and return by the next night train. Text books written by the Indian scholars were widely prescribed and used in Pakistani colleges and universities.[5] Partition and separation were accompanied by state and national identity building, conflicts, crisis and wars. The 1965 war was a turning point in terms of the openness of the countries to each other. Indian films and songs were banned from cinema houses and national radios. Borders were closed, train and ferry services were discontinued, and visa became difficult to obtain. The celebrated India-Pakistan mushairas quickly became extinct. Books, magazines and newspaper from the other country were disappeared from shelves. People and cultures were sealed off from each other. Today more than sixty five years after independence, the common people as well as the elite of India-Pakistan are questioning the wisdom of maintaining a state of confrontation, and are leaning towards establishing conditions for permanent peace. The power of the old mindset is declining; the momentum for peace is growing. Ordinary citizens in large numbers, peace activists, parliamentarians, cricketers, actors, artists, theater groups, intellectuals, journalists, women, soldiers and professionals are making a mighty contribution to peace effort. Further the India-Pakistan peace process can be categorize in three parts like, in the first part the two governments were principle actors. They talked for peace but never reached to a permanent solution. In the second part the intelligentsia in both countries started working for peace. In the third part people of the Pakistan became active

South Asia: Regional Order:

South Asia can historically seen as a contiguous civilizational area which is bound on the south by the seas and in the north by Himalayas. The eastern and the western boundaries of the region can be found in the inhospitable Karakoram and the Hindu Kush ranges in the west and the tropical forests and the Arakan Yomas in the east. The region gained unity and legitimacy over centuries through the various empires in the South Asia demarcating its geographic and civilizational reach. The British Colonial Empire (BCE) in India was probably the most hegemonic and successful in bringing this vast swathe of land under a single sovereign space.

India's defense policies and strategic vision since Independence has been tied umbilicially to the legacy of the British Empire in India. However, there were remarkable spatial differences in the post Partition Indian state and BCE and for that matter in South Asia. The strategic unity that the British gave to the subcontinent was broken in the east and the west. Second the ancient Chinese empire found its feet and, by the early 1950, was knocking on the doors of Tibet. These two factors are most crucial to understanding the challenges to the defense of India in the new geo-political world. With the Chinese integration of Tibet, the strategic insulation of South Asia from the China had changed forever.

Despite these differences with the BCE, India is the largest power in South Asia in terms of size, population and resources. India is also bigger than the rest of the South Asian states combined together. Moreover, none of the South Asian states have common boundaries with each other and India borders all the states in the region. Apart from its sheer size, the geographic constraint makes India the most important state in the subcontinent. In a region, the dominating power is expected to define the configuration of regional order according to its own ideology and identity.[6] The political elite in India has always believed that the country should aspire to be ranked among the great powers of the world with that belief anchored in its superior attributes including its geo-political status, hegemonic presence in South Asia, the perception of its potential economic and military capabilities, and civilizational ethos. In the past half a century, India has been obsessed with security concerns within the region and especially so in the smaller states like Nepal, Bhutan and Sri Lanka. In the steps towards the elusive great power status, it is very important that India manages its neighbourhood to achieve its ends and secure the region for itself.

Regional order can be maintained in two ways. The first is when the pivotal or the dominating power acts as the security manager for the entire region. The dominating power draws its legitimacy by providing public goods for the other members of the system. Such power has the potential to dramatically exacerbate the contours of conflict if disputed or challenged. In the absence of consensus and challenges to its legitimacy the region will suffer from chronic instability. In simple terms, a pivotal power gives a region cohesiveness, provides a sense of security and keep interfering external power out. The second path to regional order stems from equal powers contending with each other to maintain stability by checking each other's ambition. The Situation in South Asia is that none of these conditions holds true. Neither has India succeeded in dominating the entire region nor has the Pakistan challenge managed to countervail India's superiority. This gap between the two positions is what is responsible for the instability in the region which precludes predictable behavior or successful resolution of disputes. India's position in the region has been variously described as that of 'weak unipolarity' or 'arrested unipolarity'. The contested unipolarity has been as much a result of an underdeveloped economy as much as it has been a result of the challenge from Pakistan.

State and Nation Building in India and Pakistan:

The process of state formation and nation building in India and Pakistan were shaped by an act of surgical Partition of the Indian subcontinent. Looking back at the post second world war years, it becomes evident that the process of Partition assumed two predominant forms. The first form was related to the outcome of the Second World War as also the Cold War that eventually led to the Partition of Germany, Korea and Vietnam. The second type of partition was related to decolonization. The partition of Indian subcontinent fell into the latter category. With partition, India and Pakistan had to socially reconstruct and imagine their respective and distinct notions of national identities over the territorial states legitimized by the post partition map.[7]

After partition, there have been two dominant versions of imagining India. Out of these, the first version that upheld the notion of secular India was dominant for almost four decades after Independence. It must be that the term 'secular' appears rather vague in the Indian context. It can imply either a religion neutral state or equal respect to all religions. In fact Nehru worked tirelessly to translate their notion of secular India at the level of praxis. For instance, through memorable writings like The Discovery of India, Nehru emphasized the socially plural, inclusive, composite and tolerant character of the people and civilizations that flourished in India. He consistently reconstructed the map of India so that over 3,000 - 4,000 communities would be able to visualize the geopolitical space of India under the comprehensive umbrella of secular nationalism. Under the Nehru regime (1947-64), the immediate post partition bitterness between the Muslim and Hindu communities was overcome rather smoothly and the country plunged into the project of nation-building and modernization. As a part of social and political engineering, Nehru endeavoured to deploy the resources and manpower in India to promote gigantic developmental activities including the building of large dames like the Bhakra Nangal and steel plants like the one built at Bhilai. Simultaneously, a plethora of scientific research institutions such as the Indian Institutes of Technology (IITs) and universities were built to provide trained manpower for developmental projects.[8]

With the demise of Nehru in 1964 and the end of the one party dominant system in 1967 the notion of secular nationalism began to face increasing chalenges. The Congress regimes led by Indira Gandhi (1967-77) and (1980-84) and Rajiv Gandhi (1984-89) that succeeded the Nehru regime, did support secular nationalism, but not as convincingly as the Nehru regime. The covert support of Mrs. Gandhi to fanatic religious leaders like Bhindranwale in Punjab, for short term tactical purposes, and the susceptibility of the Rajiv Gandhi regime to the pressures of fundamentalist Muslim groups in the case of Shah Bano, a Muslim divorcee fighting for the right to receive alimony under the secular law of the land, are examples of this trend. In the process, the congress regimes could nighter evoke sympathy from the Hindu majority nor retain the support of Muslim and Sikh minorities. This paved the way for the rise of Hindu nationalism.[9]

In fact, Hindu nationalism constitutes the second important version of imagining India. The high priests of this version, such as Savarkar and Golwalkar, and their followers stood for making India a Hindu rashtra(nation). They wanted to give Hinduism a privileged position over any other religion and integrate India from the Indus to the seas on the basis of the dominant Hindu ethos. However capitalizing on the deficiencies of the secular nationalist forces led by the Congress, the Bharatiya Janta Party (BJP) and its allied parties the Sangh parivar—began to grow after the mid 1980s to contest and unmask the pseudo secularism of the secular nationalists. Events like the demolition of the Babri Masjid (1992), the rise of BJP as the single largest party in the ruling coalition in the central governments (1998-2004), the growing strenght of the Sangh Parivar and the forces of Hindu nationalism, have by now transformed the complexion of the political process in India. Moreover, as a consequence of the clash between the secular and fundamentalist forces, especially after the demolition of the Babri Masjid, the meanings as well as modes of executing secular policies have become an intensely contested area among the major political parties. Likewise, separatism in Punjab in the 1980s and ongoing separatist movements in Kashmir have once more brought home the role of religion and ethnicity in constructing modern nation states. In a word, since secularism had become a contested concept within India diverse Political forces are imagining India as an entity in different ways. Perhaps the only silver lining is that India's vibrant liberal democracy has provided a space for diverse political forces to work out the meaning and status of secularism in the changing political context. The defeat of the BJP led coalition in the 2004 General Elections, in a way, can be viewed as unwillingness on the part of the people to subscribe to the narrow agenda to the Hindutva as propounded by the BJP. Hence they voted for the forces that were closer to secular nationalism.

In contrast to India, the so called two nation theory has consistently haunted Pakistan's political evolution. In more ways than one, the birth of Pakistan was remarkable in the history of the formation of the nation states. Like Israeal, Pakistan was constituted fundamentally on the basis of religion. Obviously, the diverse linguistic communities were brought under the umbrella of Islam while constructing the notion of the nation state in Pakistan. Moreover, the areas which had a predominantly Muslim population sprang up as netural cnadidates to form Pakistan. Initially the founding fathers of Pakistan conceived of it by separating the western, eastern, and souththern parts of the subcontinent. The plans to carve out the southern wing of Pakistan through the state of Hyderabad were buried when Govt. of India under the Sardar Patel's stewardship integrated the state of Hyderabad, ruled by Nizam, with the Indian Union.[10]

Pakistan, unlike most contemporary nation states, came up as a geographically non contiguous state. Its western and eastern parts were separated by around 1400 km and these had little in common other than religion. Owing to the obvious linguistic and cultural differences between these two parts, it was difficult to bring about the national integration of Pakistan. The lack of internal cohesion virtually pushed the ruling elite in Pakistan to unite its population against an external enemy, India. The so-called inimical state of India was constructed in Pakistan through active propagation of the myth of aggressive designs of the Hindu majority in India over Pakistan. Thus, anti Indianism became one of the important planks to keep Pakistan together. By constructing the notion of Hindu India, it was also easier to invoke the bond of Islamic affinity to unify Muslims of the two wings of Pakistan. However, Pakistan's failure to keep the two wings together eventually led to the birth of Bangladesh in 1971. Owing to its bifurcation, anti Indian sentiments became more acute in Pakistan. Furthermore, unlike India, Pakistan alternated between civilian and military rule. The instability of political regimes in Pakistan further induced insecure rulers in Pakistan to invoke anti Indian stances to deflect the attention of the people from their poor performance.[11] Despite the importance of religion in daily life, urban Pakistanis overwhelmingly support the secularization of politics, the curbing of extremism, the reforms of madrasahs, and the building of relations with the west. Further in national votes, extremist parties have tended to receive negligible support. This does not mean that Islamic radicalism has no future in Pakistan. It relies primarily on the army to survive, being insufficiently popular to influence state policy through political parties or popular agitation. The army has supported it when it needed a tool to wedge its way into power but has suppressed it otherwise.[12]

India- Pakistan Peace process:

Ever since 1947, peace between India and Pakistan has been challenged by territorial disputes and competing state narratives. With the Kashmir issue at the heart of their mutual animosity, India and Pakistan fought three wars in the first quarter century of their existence. Pakistan tried to achieve its objective in 1947 by supported a tribal invasion of Kashmir, which resulted in the Kashmir war 1947-48. Pakistan tried to same objective through 'Operation Gibraltar' in 1965 and then in 1971 but failed to wrest Kashmir from India. After these invasions both India and Pakistan signed couple of agreements like Tashkent Declaration (1966) and Simla Agreement (1972) respectively to establish peace in the region. India Pakistan relation can be uncomplet without undertanding the Simla Agreement which is the benchmark of relations between these nations.[13]

Tashkent Declaration:

The second Indo-Pakistan war broke out on September 1965 over Kashmir. UN intervention brought the war to close, but the Security Council remained unable to short out their differences. The deadlock provided an opportunity for mediation to the Soviet Union. Soviet Prime Minister Alexei Kosygin had his good offices to both India and Pakistan. Both accepted this offer to end of war. Kosygin succeeded in brokering a peace agreement, as the two parties met in Tashkent in January 1966. Indian Prime Minister Lal Bahadur Shastri and Pakistan president Ayub Khan held meetings from 4 to 10 January. Kosygin stayed away from discussions for the first two days, and intervened only when he saw the summit heading for a deadlock. He held separate talks with the both leaders and finally was able to remover their differences. In an agreement signed on 10 January 1966 , both India and Pakistan declared that 'all armed personnel of the two countries shall be withdrawn not later than 25 Febreary 1966, to positions they held prior to 5 August 1965 and both sides shall observe the ceasefire terms on ceasefire line'.[14]

The Simla Agreement:

It is the simla agreement which defines the basic parameters according to which Indo-Pakistan relations have been conducted in the past, and it will be hopefully be defining the parameters in the future as well. It is therefore necessary to take a brief look at the provisions of the Simla Agreement.

The Simla Agreement desired that, the sanctity of the Line of Control (LOC) was to be maintained by the both sides and both sides agreed that 'neither side shall seek to alter it unilaterally, irrespective of mutual differences and legal interpretations.' Also there was a commitment by both countries to respect each other's 'territorial integrity and sovereignty' as well as to solve problems between the two countries by peaceful means. The two countries also agreed, 'That in accordance with the Charter of the United Nations(UN) they will refrain from the threat or use of force against the territorial integrity or political independence of each other.' The New Delhi and Islamabad also agreed that the LOC would be converted into an International border in due course. In another important clause of the Simla Agreement, both India and Pakistan, agreed to 'settle their differences by peaceful means through bilateral negotiations or by any other peaceful means mutually agreed upon between them. While the Simla Agreement can be regarded as having maintained peace between the two countries for a period of nearly two decades, that peace was broken by the Pakistan's proxy war in 1989.[15]

Relations between India and Pakistan are going through one of the worst phases ever since the signing of Simla Agreement in 1972. Indo-Pakistan relations have seen more low points in 1990 than high points in the last three decades. The political leaders of the both sides, reiterated their willingness to resume talks over the next couple of years, the atmosphere between the two countries only became conducive for such an exercise in March 1997, when Pakistan and Indian foreign secretary level talks were held in New Delhi after a long gape. Real breakthrough came in May 1997, when Indian Prime Minister I.K. Gujral met Pakistani Prime Minister Nawaz Sharif at Maldives. They took to number of decisions like agreeing to release prisoners from each other's countries, agreeing to hotline between both of them, and most importantly, agreeing to establish working group to address various outstanding issues upon which the two countries disagreed. Indo-Pak interaction acquired a new context with the nuclear tests of May 1998 when relations hit a new low. Pakistan tried to project the South Asian region as a nuclear flashpoint in the aftermath of the tests and sensitized the Kashmir question by linking it with the nuclear tests. The extreme bitterness and tension between India and Pakistan in the period after the nuclear tests did bring with it the realization on the both sides that things could not continue in the same manner indefinitely and that a meeting ground to be found. Things started looking up again as Indian Prime Minister Vajpayee met Pakistani Prime minister Nawaz Sharif at New York in September 1998. It was decided that foreign secretary level talks would be held between India and Pakistan, and a direct bus service between Lahore and Delhi was proposed.[16]

Dialogue Process in the Post Nuclear Phase:

It becomes important to take a look at the impact of the nuclear tests on the process of dialogue between the two states. In a climate of newly created tension and suspicions in the wake of nuclear tests by India and Pakistan, both countries felt the need to talk to each other at sufficiently high levels to find a meeting ground and to instill mutual confidence. The earliest opportunity available after that was at the SAARC Summit in Colombo which held in end July 1998. Both Prime Minister Vajpayee and Prime Minister Nawaz Sharif stated that they would like to utilise the opportunity to hold a meeting on the margins of the summit to have a candid exchange of views on the post nuclear security situation and if possible agree on a framework of official level talks in the near future. The deadlock in Indo-Pakistan relations was finally broken when Vajpayee met Nawaz Sharif at New York on September 1998 during the UN General Assembly session. It was agreed that two foreign secretaries would meet in Islamabad from October 1998 to focus on Kashmir and peace and security, including confidence building measures, following this there would be a series of meetings in November to discuss the six other items on the agenda. The New York meeting also resulted in a telephone hotline between two prime ministers were to be restored, trade and people to people contact were to be enhanced, the railway link between Kokrapar(Pakistan) and Munnabo(India in Rajasthan) was to be restarted and a direct bus service between Delhi and Lahore was proposed, visa rules were to be relexed, and efforts were to be made to stop cross border firing.[17]

The October rounds of talks in Islamabad did not achieve any major breakthrough, except that the process of dialogue received an impetus. India and Pakistan reiterated their known positions on Kashmir, but agreed to meet again and carry forward the dialogue at the next roung of talks between the two foreign secretaries. The Indian side proposed a no first use of nuclear weapons agreement, ensuring reliable communication links and greater transparency between the two sides through extending the hotline between the two Directors General of Military Operations to divisonal and sector, reviving the hotline between the two foreign secretaries, giving advance notice of missiles tests of over 200 km range and extending the existing agreement om non attack on each others nuclear installations to cover economic and population centers, renewal of the invitation to Pakistani Army chief to visit India and exchange of officers between the two National Defence colleges. The Pakistani side spoke of a non aggression pact, mutual nuclear and ballistic restraint while it remained cool to the no first use proposal.[18] The new delhi round of talks held in November 1998, including six issues which were Tulbul navigation project, Siachen, Sir Creek, trade, terrorism and drug trafficking and cultural exchanges.

During the talks, Pakistan rejected India's proposal for a ceasefire in Siachen,wanting instead to address the question of troop disengagement in the area. It was suggested by India that both sides could establish a 'bilateral monitoring mechanism'. New Delhi did not agree with the Pakistani proposal of placing an 'international monitoring mechanism' to supervise the ceasefire in the Siachen area.[19] The November round of talks became bogged down due to the usual accusations and counter accusations hurled by India and Pakistan towards each other. In situations they were not able to move beyond their often stated positions. However the efforts on both sides to discuss a wide range of issues was itself commendable. There was some amount of progress in the November talks which can be measured by a number of positive developments. Both countries set up technical committees on the supply of surplus power to India. Certain proposals by India to avoid double taxation were under consideration. The Pakistani proposal for setting up mechanism for quick information flows on trade and investment was agreed to by India. Pakistan agreed to ensure that visas were issued to Indians within six weeks and that there would be no delay. Both nations agreed to set up a mechanism for regular meetings and exchange of operational information between Central Bureau of Investigation (CBI) and Federal Investigating Agency of Pakistan, for expeditious assistance to each other for combating various kinds of crimes including counterfeiting of currency and cyber crimes.[20] Also there was a progress on the proposal for introduction of a bus service between Delhi and Lahore. Both countries agreed to release fishermen in each other's custody.

Lahore Bus Diplomacy:

The next landmark in Indo-Pak relations was the Indian Prime Minister Vajpayee's visit to Lahore on February 20-21, 1999 on the inauguarl run of Delhi - Lahore bus service. There was an increasing realisation on the part of both Nawaz Sharif and Vajpayee that improvement of relations between the two countries had to be a priority. The momentum for vajpayee's visit was generated when the two governments went ahead with the cricket test Serise despite right wing opposition in both countries. Also the delegation of Indian MPs to Islamabad for a parliamentarians meet organised by the Jung Group of newspaper did a fair share to promote confidence between the people of India and Pakistan. The Lahore Summit led to the signing of the Lahore Declaration by the Prime Ministers of Pakistan and India on February 21, 1999, the issuing of the Joint Statement by India and Pakistan, and the Memorandum of Understanding signed by the Foreign Secreataries of India and Pakistan. Both the Lahore Declaration and the MOU referred to mutual adherence to the principles of the UN Charter, as also contained references to the implementation of the Simla Agreement.[21] Prime Minister Atal Bihari Vajpayee and Nawaz Sharif, at the end of their summit announced a number of steps including nuclear confidence building measures, for 'prevention of conflice' between the two states. They also ageed that their respective governments reaffirmed their condemnation of terrorism and their determination to combat this problem. The two governments agreed to give advance warning to the other when conducting ballistic missile flight tests. Seeking to minimised the potential of freak nuclear accidents, the two countries agreed to alert the other immediately in case of any ' accidental, unauthorised or unexplained incedent' on the other side. The level of bilateral talks was raised to the Foreign Minister level and the composite dialogue between the two countries, foreign secretaries was to continue. While hopes were high after the summit both sides had to come down to earth soon. Nawaz Sharif could not be seen to be softening his stance on Kashmir in undue haste. The happenings in Indo – Pak relations after Vajpayee's visit give an idea of existing contradictions present in relations between the two nations. Nawaz Sharif brought up the Kashmir issue when he made a statement that Mr. Vajpayee had agreed with Islamabad's view's that the people of Kashmir should have the right of self determination. This statement was refuted by the Indian PMO. Again at Dhaka, where Nawaz Sharif had gone for the summt, he stated that 'a solution of Kashmir is a must for achieving peace in nuclearised South Asia'.[22]

While the Lahore process was the culmination of Nawaz Sharif's efforts towards taking Indo-Pak relations to a new high, it is known that the army in Pakistan was even then uncomfortable with this event, and had in the meanwhile been planning the Kargil adventure. It was reported in July 1999, that 'Highly placed sources confirm that the decision to take over the Kargil posts was taken in October last year and preparations started immediately after that'.[23] Afzal Mahmood, in his article asks the question, 'Why did Pakistan fail to give the Lahore process a good try- which means reasonable time and opportunity to prove it worth as a conflict resolution mechanism? First accept the concept of bilateralism, glorify the Lahore process and take pride in opening a new chapter in Indo-Pak relations and shortly thereafter embark upon a course of action—ill though out and rash—that brings us to an eyball to eyeball confrontation with India'.[24] The feeling of euphoria created by the Lahore Summit was completely shattered due to Pakistan's aggerssion in Kargil which marked an unanticipated downtrun in Indo-Pakistan relations.

Kargil War:

At the onset of summer in 1999, the Pakistan Army took the initiative in the Kargil Sector to start yet another war – the fourth since Independence – with India. Initially, it tried to pass it off as an extension of the ongoing proxy war in other parts of Jammu and Kashmir (J&K). Intruded in the Kargil sector were actually Pakistani regular soldiers with ambitious military objectives of (a) cutting off National Highway 1A joining Zojila to Kargil and Leh, (b) isolating and capturing Turtuk, (c) occupying part of Indian territory south of the LoC, and (d) rejuvenating militancy in the Valley which had started withering after J&K Assembly and Parliament elections. Due to inadequate intelligence and poor surveillance at the local level, it took time for the initial fog of war to clear. However, when the Indian military juggernaut got moving, it took little time to expose Pakistani lies, its operational and strategic weaknesses, and its wrong assumptions about the Indian military. Despite a self-imposed national strategy of restraint and to keep the war limited to the Kargil sector, the Indian armed forces rose heroically to the challenge and responded with a firm resolve and daring that few believed was possible. Operation Vijay was launched in May 1999 with a well-coordinated politico-military strategy. With great determination, high morale, and brilliant junior leadership, Indian forces performed gallantly. The forward movement of the Indian soldiers on the mountain tops of Kargil, one of the most difficult terrains in the world, became unbeatable and Pakistani positions fell one after another. India was able to beat back Pakistani forces on the ground and at a time of its own choosing. The Kargil war came as a great surprise and thus became a greater politico-military victory! Most of the credit for victory in Kargil will no doubt always go to the grit, determination, and dedication shown on the battlefield by our jawans and young officers.[25] As in the crisis nuclear clouds appeared to hover over the two states and intensified the tension in the region. It was feared that Pakistan would launch a pre-emptive nuclear attack. This fear was heightened when Pakistan's foreign secretary Shamshed Ahmed dropped hints of the war escalating to a nuclear confrontation. Meanwhile in the first week of July, Pakistan's Prime Minister Nawaz Sharif, under pressure from the US, promised to restore the sanctity of the LOC as per the Simla Agreement of 1972 and to re-engage in the bilateral dialogue begun in Lahore a few months earlier.[26]

The Lahore Summit would have been one of the greatest achievements throughout the history of the peace process between India and Pakistan since 1947. But in the same year (1999), india and Pakistan fought their 'fourth war' in Kargil that brought large scale violance in the region since 1971, the crisis was managed with the involvement of the US.

Agra Summit 2001:

India and Pakistan experienced the worst state of their relations after the kargil flare-up. The two countries were back to square one and withdrew their diplomatic staff from respective High Commissions. India inssited that no dialogue would take place until Pakistan stopped supporting 'cross border infiltration'. General Pervez Musharraf was not a reliable negotiator as it considered him the, 'The architect' of the Kargil war. Throughout this military deadlock, Pakistan kept on offering India negotiations at "any level, anywhere, and anytime". India rejected Pakistan's peace initiative on the basis of the Kargil conflict as well as internal political situation of Pakistan. According to an Indian analyst, "General Pervez Musharraf's capture of power in a military coup in 1999 had prompted India to declare that no India-Pakistan dialogue to resolve differences would take place till the time democracy returned to Pakistan". President Musharraf proposed a "reciprocal action plan" to implement by both countries as a first step to defuse tension and to promote peace. In May 2001, India extended an official invitation to Pakistan to revitalize bilateral contacts. In response President Pervez Musharraf accepted the invitation from his counterpart and a meeting was held between the two leaders in Agra on July 14-16 2001. The brought higher hopes to the region as it were a major breakthrough after two years stalemate. President Musharraf assured the Indian Prime Minister, Atal Behari Vajpayee, "I have come with an open mind and looks forward to my discussions with Indian leaders on establishing peaceful, tension-free and co-operative relations between our two countries". The summit despite a euphoric beginning, did not produce the desired results and was generally considered a failure.[27] But Scholars and political leaders of both the states say that the summit has not failed. At this stage the best option would be to continue bilateral negotiations with each other. In the future both the governments should try to find some meeting ground in order to pursue measures to enhance interaction and co-operation between the both nations.[28]

Attack on the Indian Parliament:

But this is evident from the fact that despite Pakistan's rebuffing of Prime Minister Atal Behri Vajpayee's Lahore peace initiative through the Kargil perfidy in 1999, he took yet another bold peace initiatives by implementing a unilateral ceasefire in Kashmir in the Islamic holy month of Ramzan in November 2000. Besides, he invited the Pakistan President, General Pervez Musharraf, for talks in the historical town of Agra in July 2001. Unfortunately, Islamabad responded to these peace initiatives by engineering attacks on the Jammu and Kashmir State Assembly on 1 October, 2001 and on the Indian Parliament House on 13 December, 2001. Being a mature and responsible nation having an understanding of the implications of war between two nuclear-armed neighbours and its international ramifications, New Delhi however rightly decided to give diplomacy one more chance even while preparing for the exercise of the last option, i.e., war. But New Delhi did give priority to diplomatic offensive, including recalling of its High Commissioner in New Delhi, terminating the New Delhi –Lahore bus service as well as Samjhauta Express, withdrawing permission to Pakistan to fly its aircraft through the Indian skies, and demanding the extradition of 20 persons accused of committing various terrorist acts in India.[29] As the Vajpayee government did not expect any voluntary action on the part of Pakistan. It banked on the moral indignation of the international community, apart from mobilizing its military forces. It held intensive consultations with leaders of important countries such as the US, Britain, Russia, Japan, and China, etc. This three-pronged Indian strategy—military build-up, mobilizing international pressure, and mounting bilateral pressure on Pakistan produce certain result. These moves not only obliged the Pakistan President, General Pervez Musharraf , to condemn religious extremism in his open address to his country on 12 January 2002, but also to ban certain terrorist outfit including Lashker-e- Toiba(LeT) and Jaish-e-Mohhamed(JeM).[30]

Peace Process back on Track:

As time move forward, Vajpayee in his speech in Srinagar on April 2003 offered the 'hand of friendship' to Pakistan and get positive response from Islamabad. The sharp transformation can be sensed in the policies of president Musharraf, who showed remarkable flexibility and innovative thinking in offering different proposal that could fulfill the aspirations of the Kashmiri people while keeping in mind the sensitivities of both

India and Pakistan. For instance, the Joint statement signed on 6 January 2004 was a serious step towards the conflict resolution between the two countries. In this statement, both states agreed to take forward and sustain the dialogue process, violence, hostility and terrorism must be prevented. On his part Musharraf reassured Vajpayee that he would not permit any territory under Pakistan's control to be used to support terrorism in any manner. He further emphasized that a sustained and productive dialogue addressing all issues would lead to positive results.[31] The Two side also took steps to appointment of high commissioners, the resumption of the Delhi –Lahore bus service, ceasefire along the LOC and along the Actual Ground Position Line(AGPL) at the Siachen glacier as well as the resumption of air links and over flights.[32] In a press conference after the release of the Joint statement, Musharraf stated: "History has been made as Pakistan and India have reached an agreement to take the process of normalization of relations forward. We have never reached the point we have reached now." Soon after the composite dialogue agreement, general elections in India led to the replacement of the NDA by a Congress-led coalition government at New Delhi in May 2004 with Dr. Manmohan Singh as the Prime Minister. Although the change in government at New Delhi was not expected to wreck the peace process, there were concerns regarding its continuity even though the Congress had backed the peace process when it was in the opposition. Moreover, Musharraf advocated a four-stage formula for the resolution of Kashmir that included, recognition of Kashmir as a dispute, initiation of a dialogue, shedding of mutually unacceptable solutions, and securing a win-win situation for all parties to the dispute. In October 2004, he proposed a three phase formula. In the first phase ethnic geographic line would be identified in Kashmir between India and Pakistan, the above regions would be demilitarized in second phase and their legal and constitutional status decided in the third and final phase.[33] In another proposal floated in 2005, Musharraf suggested "demilitarization" and maximum "self-governance" and "joint management" for Kashmir. The rationale behind these proposals was to secure a creative resolution based on concessions by all sides, yet meeting the aspirations of the Kashmiris. India rejected Musharraf's seven region proposal maintaining that it envisaged a division of Kashmir on religious lines. India's Prime Minister Manmohan Singh said: "Any proposal that smacks of a further division of our country on the basis of religion is not going to be acceptable to us." Moreover, India did not respond favorably to Pakistan's proposal on 'self governance' and 'demilitarization' and reaffirmed that there would be no redeployment of security forces while violence, terrorism and 'infiltration' continued. So the differences of opinion regarding any issue which one country considered a priority have underlined the basic dichotomy of their approaches that persists to date.[34] In April 2005, a bus line between Srinagar, the capital of Jammu and Kashmir, and the Muzaffarabad, the Capital of Azad Jammu and Kashmir (AJK) part of Pakistan Occupied Kashmir was re-established, allowing divided families to meet for the first time since 1956. After the October, 2005 earthquake in AJK region of Pakistan, India and Pakistan agreed to open the LOC at five points to facilitate the provision of humanitarian assistance as well as meetings between divided families.[35]

But in the immediate past, there have been two incidents that threatened to disrupt the peace process— the first was the attack on the make shift temple at Ayodhya on July 2005 and other was the serial blast in Mumbai on July 2006. The Indian establishment regarded both of them as 'major incidents' capable of disrupting the peace process. During the interaction with press, Prime Minister Man Mohan Singh made it clear that the success of the peace process depended public opinion and support and that an incident like the Ayodhya attack would seriously undermine the Indian government's ability to carry the people's support.[36] The Havana statement is an important marker as it came after the devastating Mumbai blasts in July 2006 which lead to the postponement of the secretary level talks. New Delhi suspended the peace process and demanded that Pakistan demonstrate its commitment to the various assurances it had given to India since January 2004. The year 2006 saw constant interaction over the working groups on the various issues agreed to in the composite dialogue process. There was a hiccup due to the Mumbai blasts but the talks continued after some damage control exercise by both countries.[37] The peace process was resumed in September 2006, when Indian Prime Minister Manmohan Singh met General Musharraf in Cuba during the Non Aligned summit where came the proposal of 'joint anti – terrorism mechanism' a non starter and produced nothing substantial for India. Further in May 2008 meeting between foreign ministers and foreign secretaries of India and Pakistan to review the 'composite dialogue' and the 'peace process' between the two adversarial South Asian neighbours appears to be reassuring. To keep the momentum of cooperation and confidence-building, especially across the LOC, the sides agreed to increase the frequency of movement of people and goods across the border through rail, road and air. Working and expert groups to explore more confidence-building measure were also be facilitated, including in the nuclear and conventional fields. The question of trade volume and imbalance were also considered and it was agreed that railway official from the two sides would meet in June 2008 to remove technical difficulties experienced in freight movement. To expend economic engagement, the two sides agreed to open the branches of each other's banks and agreed to work through the South Asian Association for Regional Cooperation (SAARC) to promote South Asian regional cooperation and development. Both sides also agreed seriously and sincerely to address the humanitarian aspects of persons of one country detained in another. An agreement was signed in Islamabad during the meeting of consular access to such detainees. There would also be release of such detainees by both the countries. The liberalization of visa regime between the two states was also reiterated.[38] November 2008 a terrorist attack on Mumbai, India blamed Pakistani based militants and freezes talks with Pakistan and Islamabad initially denied any involvement in the attacks, but in 2009 acknowledged that the assault had been partially planned on its territory and that Ajmal Qasab, the lone surviving member of the attack team, was a Pakistani citizen. It was the first time India and Pakistan have cooperated across border in the trial of terror suspects and Pakistan agreed to send a Judicial team to India during home secretary level talks but the team's arrival was delayed for some time.[39] Indian Prime Minister Manmohan Singh and Pakistani president Asif Ali Zardari met on the sidelines of an international gathering in Russia in 2009 and discussed on the issue of Mumbai terrorist attack mr. singh want him to ensure militants cannot operate from Pakistan. Indian foreign Minister SM Krishna and the newly appointed Pakistani foreign Minister Hina Rabbani Khar held talks in New Delhi in July 2011. This was a part of a series of high level meetings aimed at normalizing relations between the two states and bringing the relationship back on track.[40] They announced new Confidence Building Measures (CBMs) and expected that these will expand the scope of people to people contacts and humanitarian issues. The CBMs include increasing cross-LOC trading days and expanding travel to include tourism and religious aspects, apart from relaxing permit conditions for travel by people of Jammu and Kashmir to the other side of LOC by having a system of Six month multiple entry, To move forward and forge a cooperative relationship though they stuck to their known positions on key issues such as Kashmir and terror.[40]

In April 2012, after a long period of 7 year Pakistani president landed in Delhi for the highest level visit to India for their religious place in

Ajmer(Rajestan). The tour raised hopes that long chill in relations between the two could be close to ending because the last Pakitani leader to make the journey was President Prevez Musharraf in 2005. They agreed to move forward by liberalize trade between the nuclear neighbours and boost confidence by increasing cooperation against terrorism. Although the flying visit resulted in nothing more solid than warm words and invitation for Singh to visit Pakistan, western diplomats described it as 'good news after a lot of grim news' and said it held out the prospect of a real breakthrough in relations between the nuclear armed neighbours.[42] In August 2012 they met again on the sideline of 16th NAM summit in Tehran discussed that CBMs would help to bridge the trust deficit between the two nations. Pakistani President also reportedly invited Dr. Singh to visit Pakistan but after one day of this meeting the Indian Supreme C ourt upheld Ajmal Kasab's death sentence in the Mumbai terror attack case.[43]

After a long breakdown the newly elected prime minister of India Narendra Modi invited his Pakistani counterpart Nawaz Sharif in his oath taking ceremony with all the SAARC countries leaders and despite the immense pressure of ISI, Military Nawaz Sharif accepted the invitation from New Delhi and he came with his team in Oath ceremony of Narendre Modi and get warmed welcome from New Delhi and as well as from media of all over the world and describing this moment as 'new beginning', 'historic opportunity' ' Landmark Talks' and many more by the experts and media all over the world. Prime Minister of India Narendra Modi and his Pakistani counterpart Nawaz Sharif talked near about 50 minutes in a meeting in Hadrabad House in New Delhi on 26, May 2014 and describing the meeting 'good and constructive' and both leaders agreed to pick up the threads of the Lahore declaration, referring to a pledge both countries made in 1999 to cooperate more closely to ease tensions.[44] They also talk about terrorism and Indian Prime Minister asked that his country 'abide by its commitment' to prevent terrorism against India arising there and to speed up investigations into the 2008 attacks in Mumbai. They also discussed increasing trade and other exchanges. Sharif told reporters and said that the meeting should be 'a historic opportunity for both countries' and both leaders were elected with popular mandates and could succeed in 'turning a new page' in their countries often hostile relations and both nations shared the goal of economic development, which could not be achieved without peace and stability in the region. Both leaders agreed to change confrontation into cooperation and increase trade and people- to people contact and the foreign secretaries will stay in touch and explore how to move relationship forward.[45] They also agreed that the foreign secretaries of Pakistan and India would meet in near future. Raza Rumi, a policy analyst at Jinnah Institute in Islamabad, said Pakistanis viewed the visit as an icebreaker between the two leaders and were not expecting much more concrete progress. Although 26 May 2014th meeting was a milestone, political analysts say it is too early to say how talks between the two countries will progress. However, they say Modi's initiative in calling the Pakistani leader, and Sharif's decision to come to New Delhi, shows that both sides are willing to break the deadlock. The two rivals, who have fought three wars, have not held official talks for nearly last two years.[46]

Footnote

1. Stephen Philip Cohen, The Idea of Pakistan, Brooking Institution Press, Washington D.C., 2004, p.5.
2. Ibid, p.29.
3. V.P. Malik, Rajender Nath(ed.), Musharraf's War: Foreword, Strategic Research Center, Chandigarh, p. 250.
4. Ibid., p. 253.
5. Smitu Kothari and Zia Mian with others, Bridging Partition, People's Initiatives for Peace between India and Pakistan, Orient Black Swan, New Delhi, 2010, p.2.
6. ______
7. Rajen Harse, "India-Pakistan Conflict over Kashmir: Peace through Development Cooperation", Veena Kukreja and Mahendra Prasad Singh(eds.), Democracy, Development and Discontent in South Asia, Sage Publications, New Delhi, 2008, p.312.
8. Veena Kukreja and Mahendra Prasad Singh(eds.), Democracy, Development and Discontent in South Asia, Sage Publications, New Delhi, 2008, p.312.
9. Ibid, p.313.
10. Ibid, p.315.
11. Ibid, p.315.
12. Rafiq Dossani and Henry S Rowen(eds.), Prospects for Peace in South Asia, Satnford University Press, Stanford, California, 2005, p.2.
13. Sumita Kumar, "Trends in Indo-Pakistan Relations", Strategic Analysis, vol. 24, no. 2, May,2000, p. 224.
14. Tashkent Declaration, 10 January 1966, on www.jinnah-institute.org
15. Ibid, p.221.

16. Ibid, p.222.
17. Indian Express, September 24, 1998.
18. The Pioneer, Octobet 21, 1998.
19. The Hindu, November 7, 1998.
20. The Hindu, November 13, 1998.
21. Opcit, no. 15, p.231.
22. Times of India, March 2, 1999.
23. Newsline, July ,1999.
24. Dawn, July 18, 1999.
25. V.P. Malik, "Kargil War: Reflection on the tenth Anniversary", Strategic Analysis, vol.33, no.3, June, 2009, p. 350.
26. Gitika Commuri, "Indian Identity Narratives and the Politics of Security", Sage Publication, New Delhi, 2010, p.169.
27. Rizwar Zeb, "Peace Process and the News Media A close look at the Agra Summit", Regional Studies, Vol. 21, no.2, Spring, 2003, pp. 54-56.
28. "An official Documents on Agra Summit", Ministary of External Affairs and Defence, Government'of India, New Delhi, 2001, at http://www.mea.gov.in
29. ____
30. Nalini Kant Jha, "India and Pakistan: Prospects of War and Peace", India Quarterly, vol.58, no.2, April-June, New Delh, 2002, P.50.
31. Ibid, p.51.
32. Pakistan India Joint Statement, at www.jinnahinstitute.org.
33. Satyabrat Sinha, "The India Pakistan Peace Proecss: Incremental Progress?", Anjali Gosh, Tridib Chakarbarti and others, India's Foreign Policy, Pearson, Delhi,2009, p.231.
34. P.C. Dogra, "Change in Pak Stand on Kashmir?" The Tribune, 25 June, 2005.
35. Syed Imran Sardar, "Conflict Transformation: A Paradigm Shift in Indo-Pakistan Conflict", Regional Studies, vol.29, no.2, Spring 2011, p.25.
36. Savita Pande, "India-Pakistan Imbroglio", R.S. Yadav and Suresh Dhanda(eds.), India's Foreign Policy Contemporary Trends, Shipra Publications, Delhi, 2009, p.76.
37. The Hindu, 7 July, 2005.
38. Opcit, no.34, p.232.
39. S.D. Muni, "India-Pakistan Composite Dialogue: Towards a 'Grand Reconciliation'?", Hernaikh Singh and Tridivesh Singh Maini(eds.), South Asia in 2008 A Review, Manohar publication, New Delhi, 2009,p.414.

40. www.BBC.Com
41. Rajshree Jetly, "India and Pakistan foreign Ministers' Meeting: New Hopes and Expectations", ISAS Brief, no.209, August 2011,p.1.
42. The Indian Express, July 28, 2011.
43. www.theguardian.com
44. www.ndtv.com
45. www.edition.cnn.com
46. www.japantimes.co.jp
47. www.voanews.com

3

India Pakistan Relation and Major Issues

Pakistan political fate will also shape the regional order. If the country continues down its present pathway of violent internal discord, political turmoil, and institutional collapse, it may emerge as a greater challenge to India than the one that it currently poses. A nuclear armed neighbor and adversary facing institutional collapse can pose security challenges on an unimaginable scale because of question related to the safety and security of its nuclear arsenal. Even if the dire issues of the safety and security of its nuclear arsenal do not rise, a steady erosion of the Pakistani state may lead to the flight of refugees across a porous ,if highly militarized, international border. Such population could be transfers could be very serious demographic challenges for India and not merely in terms of sheer numbers. Instead, they could well provoke ethno religious tensions (Hindu Vs. Muslim) in extremely fraught border states that have had a history of ethno religious discord and violence. On the other hand, if democratic consolidation with Pakistan proves viable, the country may at long last be able to shed the embrace of periodic military rule. In turn, the emergence of a consolidated democratic regime may lead to the beginnings of a political rapprochement with India, there by steadily easing the long-standing hostility and competition that has characterized the relationship.[1]

India is risk-averse was amply demonstrated by India's refusal to take actions against Pakistan after the 13 December 2001 terrorist attacks on the Indian Parliament by terror groups operating from Pakistani territory. India responded to this event with the largest military mobilization in its history. However, being risk-averse owing to uncertainty about its operational successes, as well as the presence of nuclear weapons, India did not launch military actions against Pakistan. Additionally in the wake of the most audacious terror attacks in Indian history in Mumbai during 26-29

November 2008 by terror groups operating from Pakistani territory, India responded with immense restraint by giving diplomacy a chance.[2] After the 1998 nuclear test, it was initially felt that a deterrence equation might have evolved between the two countries, forcing them to abstain from full-fledged conventional wars. India – Pakistan deterrence is premised on 'existential deterrence' by which both countries are assumed to be mutually deterred by their nuclear arsenals, though neither side has declared the strength of their arsenals, thus placing their adversaries in constant doubt about their strength.

US President Obama in his very first articulation of his world view, he argued: "I will join our allies in insisting, not simply requesting, that Pakistan crack down on the Taliban, pursue Osama bin Laden and his lieutenants, and end its relationship with all terrorist groups. At the same time, I will encourage dialogue between India and Pakistan to work towards resolving their dispute over Kashmir and between."[3] Obama appears to be offering U.S. diplomatic activism on Kashmir in return for Islamabad's cooperation in fighting al Qaeda and Taliban. His argument was simple: the comprehensive normalization of Indo-Pak relations will stabilize and accelerate India's own rise as a great power.

Kashmir Issues:

Kashmir has been a bone of contention for India and Pakistan since the partition of the sub-continent in 1947. Despite the stalemate having proven costly, the two countries have failed to cooperate. Managing Kashmir militarily has been a huge burden on the economy of both countries and is also one of the biggest hurdles in their economic and social development. The Kashmir conflict is not a simple inter-state territorial dispute, which involves two clearly defined parties with two choices. Along with India and Pakistan, it involves intra-state and international actors whose role is also very important in the final outcome. The United States, China, freedom fighters, Kashmiri governments in the two parts of Kashmir, and the people of the state are the other stakeholders.[4]

Pakistan, once a part of India, is now its important neighbour but their relation has been always revolved aroud Kashmir. In the post coldwar era the situation has become more intense. The Kashmir Dispute is the center of gravity for Pakistan's Cold War with India which brought India and Pakistan very close to a third war in 1990. Many consider Kashmir the most probable nuclear flashpoint in the world today. It is worth giving a brief historical background of the dispute to understand its intractability and why an accidental nuclear exchange could erupt from it. Its origins can be traced to 1947, when subcontinent was partitioned upon the British colonial withdrawal and two independent states, India and Pakistan were created. The British succeeded in settling most territorial disputes except Kashmir. Since then, Indo-Pakistani relations have remained hostage to this problem. Immediately after independence, a war broke out between India and Pakistan over Kashmir as both wanted to take control of the territory. The war ended through a UN- mediated cease-fire agreement, but Kashmir became divided with two-thirds under Indian control and the rest under Pakistani control.[5]

India and Pakistan fought a third war in 1971. In that conflict, Pakistan lost its eastern wing, which emerged as independent Bangladesh. Following the war, the two countries signed the Simla Accord in 1972 which placed India in an advantageous position in regards to the Kashmir issue. Under the terms of the treaty, both parties agreed to settle all outstanding disputes 'peacefully through negotiations'. This, according to New Delhi, provided a new formula to settle the Kashmir dispute which fundamentally replaced the UN resolution. The Accord, in New Delhi's interpretation, ruled out extra-regional involvement in the resolution of the Kashmir dispute. Since 1972, New Delhi has used the Kashmir Accord as the main reference point to resolve the Kashmir dispute. Since 1947, New Delhi has consistently maintained that Kashmir is an Integral Part of the Indian Union. The inclusion of Kashmir within India was legitimized by the treaty of accession signed by the ruler of Kashmir Maharaja Hari Singh and New Delhi on 26 October 1947.[6]

In the India – Pakistan context, Islamists argue that Kashmir is a symbol, not the root cause of India- Pakistani conflict. They Point to General Parvez Musharraf's statement made as the chief of army staff in April 1999: "Even a settlement of the Kashmir issue will not usher in peace in the region. Low intensity conflict against India will continue because India is a large hegemonic power." This reinforces the view that the India-Pakistan conflicted is rooted in history, religion, culture and politics of revenge. There cannot be peace in the region as long as anti state actors subscribe to the Islamic caliphate and Pakistan to the two-nation theory and political power in Pakistan is exercised by the army, the mullahs and the feudal lords in the name of jihad, Islam, and Kashmir. In his book 'The Shade of Swords' a noted author and commentator, M.J. Akbar, concedes that Pakistan's anger against India is larger than the problem over Kashmir.[7]

From Lahor Agreement in 1999 until the restoration of civilian rule in Pakistan in February 2008 and Mumbai attacks in November 2008, much water has flown down the Indus. There is a perception within as well as outside Pakistan that Lahor Agreement marked the beginning of a process that led to a perceptible shift in Islamabad's approach towards Kashmir. Pakistan official policy towards Kashmir has been centered on the 47th resolution of the UN security Council. Pakistan derives its stance from its own perception of history like (a) Kashmir is the core issue, (b) the Muslim majority princely state of J&K should have naturally formed part of Pakistan, (c) India has occupied this territory by forced and fraud against the wishes of its people,(e) The Un resolutions recognize the Kashmiri people's right to self determination and etc. however there are other important elements that are left unsaid or under-emphasized, which indicate the limits of the Kashmir policy like (a) the territory to be negotiated may not include Northern Areas (Gigit, Baltistan, Huzan and Nagar), which were part of the princely state of J&K at the time of partition. (b) The term 'Kashmiri' is also not clearly defined as to whether it includes the populations from the whole of the J&K state, as it was obtained during the rule of Hari Singh, or denote only the people of Kashmiri valley, (c) the Kashmiris will exercise their 'right to self determination' only to determine Kashmir's accession to either India or Pakistan. They do not have the right to independence and etc.[8]

The Pakistan had also counted once again on internationalizing the Kashmir issue through their intervention in Kargil. Unfortunately for them, their plan backfired. The international community reacted adversely to their trans LoC adventurism and called for an immediate pullback of their forces. During their G-8 summit at Cologne in June 1999, the world leaders stopped just short of calling Pakistan an aggressor and reiterated that India and Pakistan should respect the LoC and must resolve their problems bilaterally through dialogue. The G-8 statement amounted to strong indictment of Pakistan's transgression of the LoC. What came as an even greater shock to Pakistan was that China, a long –time ally, chose to adopt a strictly netural position on the Kargil intrusions and steadfastly refused to back Pakistan despite personal visits to Beijing by the Pakistani prime minister, foreign minister and chief of army staff. Once the major world powers expressed their support for India, by tacit implication even if not in a forthright manner, India has categorically stated that there can be no political negotiations with Pakistan till the intrusions in Kargil district are completely eliminated. The world is gradually coming around to accepting this justifiable Indian view. [9]

Kargil crisis put the international community on a sharp alert, particularly due to the prospects of nuclear conflagration. Fearing that the situtation could spin out of control, western governments, the UN, Japan and Russia urged caution and appealed to the two sides to pull back. International concern focused on protecting the fledgling confidence building measures, which were set up in Lahore Summit.[10]

In an unending conflict, players cannot be sure when the last interaction between them will take place. In such a situation, cooperation is quite probable. Kashmir also appears to be an unending conflict. For over 60 years, both India and Pakistan have mostly adopted the defection strategy, playing the PD game as a chess game. However, the realization has recently dawned upon the leadership of India and Pakistan that if they continue fighting over Kashmir in the same manner, it will lead them nowhere. It appears from the developments in the last decade or so that the leadership in both countries has realized that total victory is not possible, even in a distant future and they cannot run away from the dispute either.[11]

Kashmir is obviously a potential tar pit for U.S. diplomacy, Obama mused about a fundamental change in the regional dynamic. He said "working with India and Pakistan to try to resolve the Kashmir crisis in a serious way" is one of the "critical tasks" for his administration. Obama lays out the kind of reasoning the special envoy could use in New Delhi and Islamabad. According to the new US president, the envoy needs to ask the Indians why do they "want to keep on messing with Kashmir" when they are on the brink of becoming an economic superpower? To the Pakistanis, the envoy could say, "look at India and what they are doing, why do you want to be bogged down with Kashmir." An Indian hesitation regarding Obama's appointing a special envoy on South Asia and Kashmir, External Affair Minister Pranab Mukharjee in New Delhi was compelled to reject any mediatory effort by the United States. According to one analyst, Lisa Curtis, "more effective approach would recognize that Pakistan's focus on Kashmir is a symptom of border issues, including the impact of India's emergence as a global power and the Pakistan Army's continued domination over the country's national security policies."[12]

The Indus water treaty and dispute:

In the 19th century, the british constructed most of what is today the worlds largest contiguous irrigation system in the Indus Basin. However, the boundries between the two states drawn in 1947 paid no attention to hydrology. Seeing that India and Pakistan were unable to resolve this issue, the world bank offerd its help. After 10 years of intense negotiation, in 1960 the Indus Water Treaty(IWT) was signed by then Indian Prime Minister Jhawaharlal Nehru, Pakistani President Ayub Khan and the world Bank.[13] The treaty consist of a Preamble, 12 article and 8 annextures of a technical nature. There are foure essential elements to the treaty. The first relates to the divison of the waters. The waters of the three major western rivers(the Indus, the Jhelum and the Chenab) were allocated to Pakistan, and the waters of the three eastern rivers(the ravi, the Beas and the Sutlej) were allocated to India. The second main features of the treatya are that two countries would regularly exchange data, regarding the water flow withdrawal. Other main feature was finincing plan for the Indus Basin Development for irrigation and other related works.[14] The fourth element of the treaty is the dispute resolution mechanism, which sets up rules whereby first recourse is for the Indian and Pakistani IWT commissioners to resolve potential problems. If this fails then there are provisions for external arbitration, either through a netural expert appointed by the world Bank, or through an International court of arbitration.[15] The first conflict regarding IWT emerged in 1970, when India proposed to counstruct a Salal Dam over river Chenab, Pakistan protested project of Salal Dam. It objected to the design and storage capacity of the Dam. The Indian side shown flexibility in reaching an understanding and decided to alter the design of Dam. Finally an agreement was made and the acceptance of each other's problem, could also be seen in this agreement. It shows a high level of understanding from both side.

The Baglihar Case:

The different views of Islamabad and New Delhi first came to head after the India started constructing the 450 megawaat(MW) Baglihar project in 1999 on the chenab river. Pakistan belived that Indian design violated the IWT because the dam included gated spillways which mean that the manipulable stroage was larger than that allowed under the IWT. Indian view was that if they were unable to operate the reservior more flexibly, it would rapidly fill with silt. As happened earlier in the Salal Project. The Indian and Pakistani IWT commissoners were unable to resolve the difference with pakistan asking the World Bank to appoint a Netural Expert(NE) in 2005. Turning to the finding of the NE on the Baglihat differences. The NE gave precise answer in 2007 to the specific question put to him, based on the existing treaty provisions. He accepted the design flood proposed by India, considered gated spillways necessary in the circumstances of the case, upheld the placement of the gates, slightly raised the placement of the water intake, made a small reduction in the capacity of the pondage, correspondingly raised the dead storage level, and slightly reduced the freeboard. The one new element that the NE introduced was his stress on the need for periodical flushing of the reservior for desilting purposes.[16]

In August-October 2008, a huge controversy erupted over the initial filling of the completed Baglihar reservior. Major deviations from the treaty provisions were alleged, the general impression was created that India had stopped the flows of the Chenab and caused serious harm to Pakistan, and mala fides on the part of India were implied if not explicitly attributed. There was genuine bewilderment and dismay in India early in 2009 when the water issue was projected by Pakistan as a major one between the two countries, and given the same salience as Kashmir. In the Past, official Pakistani criticisms about particular Indian projects such as Baglihar had found echoes in the media and even in civil society, but no one attributed water shortage in Pakistan to Indian wrongdoing, and no one side "India is stealing Pakistan's water." This is a new very recent phenomenon, and it has rapidly spread and now forms the general climate of opinion in Pakistan, undoing years of patient work in both countries to promote goodwill and understanding.[17] This is now a closed issue. At a recent meeting of the Indus Commission, Pakistan is reported to have said that it would not pursue the Baglihar filling issue any further, and India is reported to have said tht it would evolve a proper consultation procedure to obviate such controversies in he future.

Pakistani worries about a present or impending water scarcity and the readiness to believe that India has something to do with it, and its apperehensions about the cumulative impact of planned Indian projects on the western rivers, may be well founded or baseless, but they have the potential of causing serious strains in the relationship between the two countries at every level. India needs to dispel misperceptions, if any, reassure Pakistan that it has no intention of harming that country, and if necessary, undertake some joint studies. Those efforts have to be made at both official and non official levels.

The Siachen Glacier dispute:

Siachen Glacier, the highest battle field in the world, is one of the most unfriendly and glaciated regions of aggression. Originating in the Karakoram Ranges, the glacier is 76 kilometers long and varies in width between 2 to 8 kilometers. Hostile weather conditions bear serious consequences for the troops in the area, as only 3 percent of the Indian casualties have been caused by enemy dismissal. The rest 97 percent succumb to altitude, weather, and terrain. Fortunately, guns have been silenced in the area since the ceasefire was effected in 2004. India and Pakistan were close to an agreement in 1989 but eventually failed to sign it, largely due to India's domestic political compulsions. Elections were round the corner and Rajiv Gandhi's Congress regime was opposed to troop withdrawal in an election year. Since then adverse slides in Indo-Pak relations, primarily due to militancy in J&K, has lowered trust levels between the two parties negating any compromise solution in the dispute. Proposals on prospective solutions have ranged from demilitarization, joint monitoring, to turning it into a peace park. The basic dispute at present hinges on India insisting on authentication of the current troops positions before any withdrawal is undertaken and Pakistan refusing the proposal fearing that it may amount to a formal acknowledgement of India's occupation of the current positions. In recent years, back channel diplomacy has renewed hopes of a compromise. India of late has begun consider a withdrawal, unlike before, subject to assurances that vacated positions would not be reoccupied by Pakistan. Similarly, Pakistan has moved away from its claim on an unconditional withdrawal and started to accommodate India's concern without undermining its own official stand on the dispute[18]. The talks on Siachen restarted at the Defence Secretary level in August 2004 which proved comprehensive, apart from agreeing to hold further talks on the dispute. The Foreign Secretaries of Indian and Pakistan met on 4 September 2004 in New Delhi again to discuss the eight baskets of issues including Siachen. These review talks were focused more on the progress made so far rather than discussing the technicalities involved in them. The ninth rounds of discussions were held between Defence Secretaries level at periodic intervals in 2005 in which the two sides failed to produce anything substantial on Siachen[19]. In 2006, Defence Secretary level talks on Siachen were held on 22_23 May in New Delhi again with no substantial progress made besides agreeing to continue with the ceasefire and holding further talks. The issue was again up for discussion during the Foreign Secretary level meetings on 14_15 November 2006 in New Delhi. Again the basic contention over the confirmation of troop positions on the glacier hampered any progress. In a recent significant development, Pakistan proposed a "middle way". It offered to "acknowledge" the current position of the Indian troops rather than "authenticate" it, which suggested a unspoken acceptance of India's claim over Siachen[20]. The proposal is insincere with the Indian government which is giving it serious consideration and discussing the technicalities involved in detail.

The Sir Creek dispute:

Sir Creek, an unpredictable tidal channel, is a sixty-mile-long estuary in the swamps of the Rann of Kutch between the Indian state of Gujarat and the Pakistani province of Sind. Originally an extention of the Arabian Sea, The Rann area was closed off and got converted into a salty marsh.[21] It forms part of the once disputed Rann of Kutch Area in the Western Sector of India, which was settled through the Indo-Pakistani Western Boundary Case Tribunal's Award on 19 February 1968. The Tribunal excluded the Creek saying that it was out of the purview of the Tribunal. The present dispute areas on the demarcation of the boundary from "the mouth of Sir Creek to the top of Sir Creek" and from "the top of the Sir Creek eastwards to a point (on land) preferred as the Western end." The boundary thereafter has been fixed. The determination of the boundary in the Creek area remains under dispute due to differences over whether the creek falls under the 'Thalweg' principle, which provides for making the mid-channel as the boundary. India argues it's a navigable creek which is disputed by Pakistan. Pakistan says that the boundary lies on the eastern side and therefore the creek is Pakistan's which is disputed by India claiming that the boundary lies in the middle of the creek. Determination of the boundary in the Creek area enlarges the Exclusive Economic Zone (EEZ) of either side by 250 sq. miles making it a territorial-cum-resource dispute, and that's why the deadlock. Pakistan also insists that the boundary in the Creek first be delimited in order to establish the point on the land from which a sea boundary can be delimited. India's concerns centre on the delimiting of the maritime boundary first and then moving towards the land. Both sides are keen to settle the dispute which would enable them to undertake oil and gas exploration. Several rounds of talks have been held since 1989 to settle the matter but with little success. In recent years both sides have shown seriousness in settling the matter to escape the United Nations Convention on the Laws of the Sea (UNCLOS) which would declare the area as international waters should the two sides fail to determine their claims for respective maritime zones by 2009[22]. Following the revival of the peace process, the first round of talks were held on 6_7 August 2004 led by Indian Surveyor General Prithvish Nag and Pakistan's Additional Secretary of Defence Admiral Ahsan ul Haq Chaudhary to apprise each other with the ground situation and respective views on how to resolve the dispute[23]. As a part of the peace process, technical level talks on Sir Creek were held on 22_23 December 2006 in Rawalpindi and the decision was taken to hold a joint survey of the Sir Creek and adjoining areas by the hydrographers and also simultaneously undertake discussions to determine the maritime zones of both countries. The Joint Survey was complete by mid- March 2007 to verify outermost points of coastlines using the equidistance method. Following the joint survey, talks were held in Rawalpindi, Pakistan on 17_18 May 2007 which proved inconclusive. The difference persisted over whether the boundary lay in the middle or on the eastern bank of the Creek. The two sides agreed to hold further talks to settle their differences.[24] The Sir Creek dispute too, like the Tulbul/ Wullar dispute is very much a tractable matter and can be resolved through a compromise. The basic problem is that those at the centre of the dispute on both sides and the decision-makers appear unwilling to make any compromises which are not very cordial and friendly at the moment.

Wullar Barrage Storage/Tulbul Navigation Project:

India and Pakistan deviate even on the name of this dispute. India refers to it as Tulbul Navigation Project whereas Pakistan calls it the Wullar Barrage. The basic dispute is over a barrage that is to be constructed by the government of the Indian state of Jammu and Kashmir on the Jhelum River just beneath Wullar Lake situated about 25 kilometers north of Srinagar on the river Jhelum at about 5,180 feet above sea level.[25] The name Wullar derived from the Sanskrit word "woll" meaning "obstacle". Pakistan's contention is that the Wullar Lake site is not suitable for a dam of any size as it would flood Srinagar and the Valley. India argues that it would be used to maintain navigability in the Jhelum River during lean months. India vacant the construction work until a contract was reached through direct talks and discussions. Ten rounds of talks have already been held to resolve the issue but with little progress. The talks restarted at the secretary level between the India Ministry of Water & Power and the Pakistani Ministry of Water Resources on 29_30 July 2004 in which the two sides looked at the issue in light of the provision of the Indus Waters Treaty of 1960. The talks were cordial but failed to yield any breakthroughs. In 2005, the next round of talks between the two ministries looked into the clash, laying down future courses of action but like the previous round no concrete solution emerged. It is important to highlight that the term 'Storage Project' has been added to the arrangement at Pakistan perseverance, making the technical name read as 'Wullar Barrage & Storage Project/ Tulbul Navigation Project'. In June 2006 secretary level delegations from both sides looked into the clash using the 1960 Indus Waters Treaty as the guiding principles for their exercise. There was no progress made and the dispute awaits further talks.[26] The dispute is mainly a resource issue, but due to its location in J&K, it becomes a politically sensitive issue for both sides. Technically speaking the dispute is not difficult in nature and it is the connection with the Kashmir issue perhaps which delays any progress on the matter. This dispute can be resolved of it can be de-linked from the larger issue of Kashmir and be taken as purely a resource dispute.

Terrorism Issues

The origins of state sponsored terrorism in Pakistan could be traced to Soviet Military intervention in Afghanistan in 1979. Soviet intervention in Afghanistan weakened the US presence in the region. In these circumstances Saudi Arabia and Pakistan became US allies in its mission to repel the Soviet invasion of Afghanistan. The US provided technology and sophisticated weapons, Saudi Arabia provided money and Pakistan became a hub for recruiting and training Mujahedeen groups.[27]

In December 1999, an Indian Airlines flights was hijacked and taken to Kandahar, Afghanistan, then under Taliban rule. Buckling under domestic pressure, New Delhi agreed to free three Pakistani terrorists in exchange for the passengers and crew aboard the aircraft. One of the three, Mulana Masood Azhar, later founded Jaish-e- Muhammed, the Pakistani based terrorist outfit which claimed responsibility for the attack on the Indian Parliament in December 2001. Another Ahmed Omar Saeed Sheik, was later arrested for the slaying ofWall Street Journal reporter Daniel Pearl. The third, Mushtaq Ahmed Zargar, runs military training camps in Kashmir. In July 2000, a summit between Vajpayee and Musharraf ended with the latter walking away in a huff. In December 2001, Pakistani terrorists attacked the Indian Parliament. India responded by mobilizing for war, but stood down in June 2002 after intense international pressure. In 2003, the two sides agreed to ceasefire along the LoC. The July, 2006 Mumbai train bombings killed 207 people and injured over 700. That bombings also like bear a connection to the intractable Kashmir dispute between India and Pakistan: though a group calling itself Lashkar-e-Qahhar claimed responsibility in an email to a local telivasion station.[28] In November, 2008

Pakistani terrorist struck India's financial capital, Mumbai, Killing 166 people in Multiple locations. Investigations into Mumbai's 26/11 attack made startling revelations about the militant training camps in Pakistan-occupied Kashmir (PoK). The Mumbai perpetrators started from Baitul-Mujahideen in Muzaffrabad, the capital of so-called 'Azad kasmir', and headed for Mumbai via Karachi. They underwent specialized training in PoK for an extended period before the attack. Over the years, PoK has become a safe haven not only for terrorist operating in Kashmir but also for those linked with international terror outfits like Al Qaeda. At least 55 training camps are said to be located in the region and their cadre numbers close to 5000. Muzaffarabad and Kotli are known epicenters of such camps. There are reports that these terrorist camps recruit women cadres to deceive the Indian security forces as they pass off as locals. They tactic was adopted after the Indian forces foiled a number of infiltration attempts by these groups. The women cadres undergo tough training in the handling of arms and guerrilla warfare in the PoK region.[29]

The proliferation of militant camps in PoK could also be attributed to the absence of socio – economic development. These clandestine activities thrive on the small economic incentives which terrorist groups provide to lure the people. An appalling fact that emerged during the interrogation of Mohammed Ajmal Kasab, the lone surviving terrorist of the Mumbai carnage, is that his family, which is very poor, was given Rs. 1 lakh in exchange for his inclusion in the group. Militants in training camps are paid as Rs. 1000 per month along with food and clothing. Problems in PoK are multi-dimensional, there is poverty, unemployment, and an acute sense of alienation amongst the people. Most significantly, there is a lack of political will in Pakistan for the betterment of PoK because there has been a titular political structure which is totally in effective.

In India the mood was ugly. Well connected Indian former officials who informally advise the government made clear that they supported the government's decision not to take military action after Mumbai, but that "another Mumbai" might tilt the decision in the other direction. Indian across the board are convinced that ISI backed the Mumbai attacks, and that the distinction between current and former ISI officers is meaningless. The former GOP reply, which did acknowledge that Pakistani soil was used, came as pleasant surprise, and reduced the calls for vigorous counter action.

Indian calling for a more muscular reaction to the attacks on Mumbai lack good military options. Former military and intelligence officers grumble that India needs better capabilities and options. The nature of these options remains imprecise. One retired senior official spoke of a strategy of "keeping Pakistan guessing" in which India would move troops but not tanks along the India-Pakistan border, rev up intelligence operations in Balochistan, fly military aircraft close to (but not over) the border in short, keep Pakistan off balance without impelling it to respond militarily. The assumption behind this thinking is that India knows exactly how far it can push Pakistan.[30]

Drug Trafficking:

Pakistan has become a part of the Golden Triangle notorious for poppy cultivation and illegal traffic in drugs along with Iran and Afghanistan. Although the Zia ul- Haq regime declared the use of opium illegal in Pakistan in 1979 but drug related farming still continue there in Baluchistan and North West Frontier Province (NWFP). The ISI (Inter Service Intelligence) actively indulged in drug smuggling for laundering money to meet the expenditure on war fronts in Afghanistan and India. The Indo-Pak border became vulnerable to transactions in arms and drugs. The drug barons in Pakistan rooted these items through the states of Punjab, Rajasthan, and Gujarat. With the fencing of the border in Rajasthan and Punjab the ISI had to shift the bases of its operations. By now it has been able to establish bases in Myanmar, Bangladesh and Nepal through narcotic funds. The drug dealers have opened many other different through Centeral Asian Republics(CARs) and become a global network.[31] Hence apart from the states on Indo-Pak border such as J&K, Punjab and Rajasthan, India's north eastern states including Assam, Manipur, and Nagaland have become vulnerable.[32]

Missile Programs of India-Pakistan:

Over the Past decade India has pursued an active missile programme with the help of the United States, Israel and Russia. It also develops the system indigenously. India's decision to acquire missile defences was based on its viewpoint on nuclear weapons and deterrence. It already has an advanced and well- developed ballistic missile programme, as well as nuclear warheads to arm the missile. At present India has missile capability which can target not only all of Pakistan's territory, but also able to target all of Chinese territory and beyond. On the other side Pakistan too has a well developed missile programme based on its viewpoint on security threat comes from India. The prime objective of Pakistan's Ballistic missile force is to provide a reliable delivery system for its nuclear warheads in order to India's conventional or WMD(weapons of Mass destruction) attack. Pakistan's ballistic missile play an important role in its deterrence strategy, though its ability to produce its own missile system is extremely limited both for the technological and economic reasons. At present the ratio of India's superiority over Pakistan is probably 2 to 1 in nuclear warheads and 3 to 1 in ballistic missile.[33]

India: Ballistic missile capabilities:

India has developed a ballistic missile production capability. India's missile programme has benifited from both direct and indirect assistance from nations like France, Germany, Russia, the United States and Israel. India has placed high priority on creating an independent military missile programme which will ultimately make it self sufficient in the design and production of a full range of missiles, from anti tank and surface to air missile, and perhaps even through intermediate range ballistic missiles (IRBMs). It has developed a short and medium range capability, which includes Prithvi and Agni series. India has developed SRBMs and IRBMs not only to deter a potential nuclear strike from Pakistan but also to counterbalance the nuclear threat from China. The following is a summary of India's current ballistic missile and space launch vehical programmes and provides an assessment of the missile that nation could be developing.[3.4]

Prithvi Series: Prithvi is the nuclear capable surface to surface missile is built by bharat Dynamic Ltd.(BDL),the single stage liquid fuel missile. In India has Prithvi I It can carry a 1000 kg payload up to 150 Km., Prithvi II a 250 Km version it can carry 500 kg payload. Both the version currently in services with the Indian armed forces. According to the Defence Research and Development Organization (DRDO), four different types of warhead have been developed for Prithvi. India has reportedly also planned the development of the Prithvi III, a 350 Km. boosted liquid fuel system. Agni Series: In 1994, the United states persuaded India to suspend testing of the 2500 Km Agani missile after three test flights. The missile used an Indian SLV 3 booster for its first stage and solid fuel for its second stage. India claims that this missile will be used only to carry a conventional warhead, the cost of warhead cannot be justified unless used as a nuclear delivery vehical. In April 1999 India tested Agani II , an intermediate range nuclear capable ballistic missile. The missile is based on powered by entirely by solid fuel and have a mobile launch capability. It also equipped with a global positioning system(GPS). The 20 meter long missile cal carry a 1000 kg payload 2000 Km. Agni II was design to carry a nuclear warhead if required. Further India is moving ahead with aimed at improving range and efficacy if it. India last tested the Agni III's 3500 Km range in 2007, which effectively brought distant Chinese cities and infrastructure within range for the first time, alternating the balance of power in the region. The Agni IV, missile is at the design stage and work is in progress with a 6000 Km rang, would effectively bring China's capital Beijing and also European continent into rang of Indian missile. Surya: India could be developing a 5000 Km range Surya(meaning Sun in Sanskrit and many other Indian Language) ballistic missile capable of striking targets in the continental United States. The Surya is an unconfirmed programme that has been mentioned in the Indian press. It was started in 1994 and the missile is modeled on Polar Satellite Launch Vehicle(PSLV). India has continued to produce and all test all five of the missile being developed under its Integrated Guided Missile Development Programme(IGMDP). Dhanush: A naval version of the Prithvi, 8.5 meter Long Dhanus was tested in 2000 from a ship anchored 20 Km offshore in Bay of Bengal. Sagarika: The New York Times reported in April 1998 that Russia was helping India build a nuclear capable sea launched missile called Sagarika (Oceanic). Both India and Russia denied cooperating on the project, but India reportedly confirmed latter that its Aeronautical Development Establishment(ADE) was developing a 300 Km cruise missile. It is possible that Sagarika will be deployed on the Advance Technology Vessel(ATV), India's nuclear power submarine, which is under development with Russian assistant.[35]

India's ballistic missile defence options:

At present, India's ballistic missile defence plans have revolved around the evaluation of three distinct system: the Israeli Arrow, The Russian Antey 2500/ S-300VM and the Russian Almaz S 300, PMU 1/ 2 Moreover, India has made tentative requests for information on the American Patriot PAC 3. The American Patriot system has been initially designed as an antiaircraft system. As discussed earlier, India has adopted two ways for the acquisition of missile defence system, first acquiring from abroad and second to develop the system indigenously. In this effort the developments are as following:

Trishul: Trishul is a short range, quick reation, all weather surface to air missile designed to counter a low level attack. In fact Trishul was one of the long running DRDO missile developments programme. It can also be used as an anti sea skimmer from a ship against low flying attacking missile. The missile can engage targets like aircraft and helicopters, flying between 300-500 m/s by using its radar commando line of sight guidance. Powered by a two stag solid propellant system similar to the ones used in the Patriot. Trishul with its advance technology providing considerable advantage to the Indian armed forces. Akash: The Akash system is a medium range surface to air missile with multi target engagement capability. It can carry 55 kg multiple warhead capable of targeting five aircraft simultaneously up to 25 km and is said to be comparable to the US Patriot as an air defence missile.[36] Nag: Another missile under IGMDP is the Nag, an anti-armour weapon employing sencer fusion technologies for flight guidance. The Nag is third generation 'fire and forget' anti tank missile in India with a range of 4-8 km. Nag uses imaging infra red (IIR) with day and night capability. Nag was successfully test fired in 2008 marking the completion of the development test.

It would be apposite to conclude by stating that India's missile programme represent an iconic image demonstrating sovereignty and self reliance vis-à-vis its technological achievements. Result of nearly three decades of research, India's guided missile programme has assumed a self sustaining character and become fundamentally crucial to its proposed deterrent.[37]

India's Cruise Missile:

India is expected to significantly enhance its long range strike abilities with the BrahMos supersonic cruise missile, jointly developed by New Delhi and Moscow. It derives its name from the Brahmaputra and Moscow rivers in both countries- has a range of almost 300 km with warheads up to 200 kg in weight and designed for use with land, sea and air platforms. The missile can fly at 2.8 times the speed of sound and it is highly accurate and can be guided to its target mainly with the help of an onboard computer. Both army and navy are inducting the BrahMos missile. While army had ordered two BrahMos regiments with 134 missile and navy had ordered 49 BrahMos firing units and ordered 240 missile.[38] Yet another cruise missile, the Nirbhay was announced in 2007- a subsonic missile with a range of 1000 km. capable of being launched from multiple platforms on land, sea, and air. Nirbhay will be a terrain hugging, stealth missile capable of delivering 24 different types of warhead depending on mission requirements and will use internal navigation system for guidance. In fact, Nirbhay will supplement BrahMos in the sense that it would enable delivery of warheads farther than 300 km range of BrahMos.

Delhi has also taken steps towards achieving submarine launched ballistic missile capability, with the first test of K-15(Sagarika) taking place in 2008 from a submerged barge with a range of 750 km., the Sagarika missile is being integrated with India's nuclear powered Arihant class submarine that began sea trials in 2009. According to an Indian official "Every modern military needs to have missile options. The requirements for Nirbhay were projected by all three armed forces to fill a gap in Indian missile programme. He said would weigh around 1000 kg and travel 0.7 mach (nearly 840 km/h) and would be capable to 24 different types of warheads."[39]

Pakistan's ballistic missile programme:

Pakistan's missile development programme is like its nuclear programme has been driven entirely by its security concern vis-à-vis an increasingly militaristic and bellicose India, which seeks, without any pretence, a regional and global power status. Pakistan has been a reluctant entrant into the missile club and reiterated on a number of occasions that it has no intention of matching India for missile and has deliberately eschewed a nuclear / missile arms race with India by embracing a policy based on "Minimun Nuclear Deterrence". Pakistan has a well developed ballistic missile programme. However, unlike India , whos developments of missile based power projection capabilities reflects both regional and extra regional security concern, Pakistan ballistic missile effort is largely Indo-centric. Pakistan embarked on indigenous ballistic missile effort with the launch of the Hatf programmein early 1980s. The Space and Upper Atmosphere Research Commission (SUPARCO) under took then programme. The existence of the missile was publically disclosed by Pakistan's then army staff General Mirza Aslam Beg in 1989.

Hatf-1, 1A, & Hatf-2 missiles:

The Hatf-1 is a single stage solid motor missile capable of delivering a 500 kg payload over a maximum range of 60-80 km. A subsequent version, Hatf-1A, was tested in 2000 and is believed to have an extended range of 100 km., the Hatf-2(Abdali), is a two stage solid motor missile that reportedly has a throw weight of 500 kg over a maximum range of 290-300 km. All version of the Hatf, 1, 1A, and 2, are capable of delivering conventional high explosive warheads. Some analysts speculate that the Hatf, 1, 1A and 2 use an internal guidance system. But the US government sources contend that the missile are essentially inaccurate battlefield rockets.[40] Hatf-III(Ghaznavi) is a short range, solid propellant, road mobile, single warhead ballistic missile. The Pakistan Army conducted a launch of the Ghaznavi in 2003 and again tested in 2006 to validate the missile's various designs parameters. Subsequently in 2004, the then president Pervez Musharraf formally inducted the missile in to the Army's Strategic Forces Command. Hatf-IV(Shaheen-I) is a single stage, solid propellant, road mobile, short range ballistic missile. It can deliver a 500 kg warhead over a range of 600 km. Other reports suggest that with a smaller warhead, the missile could have a range of 800 km. Pakistani governments statements suggest that the missile in Pakistan's Possession have a maximum range of 700-800 km., but the missile's payload capacity at that range remains unclear. Since then, then the missile has been in possession of the Army's Strategic Forces Command(ASFC) even as the routine test of missile have been conducted. Hatf-VI(Shaheen II) is a two stage solid fuel missile with a range of 2000 km. Development flight test of the missile began in march 2004 when a 26 ton missile was launched from Pakistan's Sonmiani Flight Test Range on the Arabian sea. According to the Chairman of Pakistan's National Engineering and Scientific Commission(NESCOM), Dr. Samar Mubarakmand, the missile covered a distance of 1800km during the test. The missile was tested in 2005, 2006, 2007 and in 2008, Pakistan tested the Shaheen II twice in three days.[41] Ghauri-I & Ghauri-II, III : Pakistan's liquid engine ballistic is spearheaded by the Khan Research Laboratory(KRL) and built on collaboration with North Korea. Ultimately, Pakistan flight tested a North Korean missile Nodong, which was re named Ghauri in 1998. Pakistan has come a long way in its missile development efforts and has acquired the capability to produce short and medium range ballistic missile of both liquid and solid fuelled varieties. The test firing of the liquid fuelled Ghauri, with the range of 1500 km contributed significantly to enhancing Pakistan's deterrence and providing it with a capability to match India's Agni missile which has tested several year earlier. In response to the India's Agani II it was designated as Ghauri-II with a range of 2500km. Pakistan is also developing Ghauri III version in response to the Indian Agani III, which will have a range of 3000km.[42] However, as a result of a conscious decision and acting in a responsible and restrained manner, Pakistan has broken out of the action reaction syndrome, which earlier characterized the relations between the two South Asian neighbours.

Pakistan's Cruise missile:

Babur: named after the first Mugal Emperor Zaheerud Din Babur also designated as Hatf VII, is the first land attack cruise missile to be developed by Pakistan. Launched from ground based transporter eractor launchers, warships, submarines and aircraft, Babur can be armed with a conventional or nuclear warhead and has and has a reported range of 700km. the missile is designed to avoid radar detection and penetrate enemy air defences. Serial production of the babur started in October 2005. It has been reported that babur is based on the American BGM 109 Tomahawk cruise missile. The Babur's airframe is made up of a tubular fuselage, with a pair of folded wings attached to the middle section and it has maximum speed of about 550mph. More advance version of the Babur are under development. Latter version are planned to have a range of 1000km and capable to being launched from submarines.[43] Two year after the first testing Babur , Pakistan test fired a new air launched cruise missile, the Ra,ad(Arabic for Thunder), on July 2007, from a Mirag III EA aircraft of the Pakistani Air Force(PAF). This nuclear capable missile reportedly has a 350 km range along with stealth capabilities. Although the first test of the Ra,ad took place from Mirage aircraft, one analyst opined it was probable that Ra,ad would be deployed on the F-16 and F-16C fighters.[44]

Nuclear issues:

While many strategic analysts in India adopted a hopeful view that the addition of offsetting nuclear weapon capabilities might stabilize relations with Pakistan. The term nuclear strategy is used here in the broad sense of exploiting nuclear weapons for both political and military purposes. It includes component strategies for deterrence, crisis bargaining, and employment. In addition, in the case of India and Pakistan, both of which are not genuinely autonomous actors in the nuclear field, there is an important component of strategy that is aimed at influencing global opinion. The nuclear strategies of both countries emphasize the deterrence, but there is a fundamental difference between the two in that Pakistan's strategy is aimed at deterring a conventional threat from India, while India's aimed at deterring a nuclear one from Pakistan. Since a conventional confrontation is easier to develop and must almost invariably precede a nuclear one, Pakistan's deterrence has to function much more actively than India's. The India-Pakista nuclear balance have argued India has been ahead of Pakistan for several decades. This may or may not be correct today. Because three possibilities exist for the Indo-Pak nuclear balance. India and Pakistan may be approximately equal. India may be ahead by as much as 60 to 100. Alternatively, Pakistan may be ahead by as much as 100 to 60. Important conclusions can be drawn from this assessment. If India is ahead of Pakistan or Pakistan is ahead of India in quantitative terms, the differences are relatively small. They are insignificant in terms of military power or deterrence impact. This has an impact on the force structure, the force posture, and the relationship between conventional and nuclear strategies.[45]

India exploded its first nuclear device, code-named 'Buddha Smile' on 18 May 1974 at Pokhran. New Delhi claimed it was a 'Peaceful Nuclear Explosion(PNE) with no military implications. But Pakistan and Western countries disputed India's claim. The latter imposed punitive sanctions on India in reaction to this explosion. Islamabad, meanwhile, considered the 'Buddha Smile' as a threat to its very survival and an instrument of 'blackmail'. The Pakistani prime minster Bhutto described India's explosion as part of an Indian effort to intimidate Pakistan and solemnly pledged that 'It (Pakistan) would not accept under any circumstances India's hegemony over the subcontinent'. New Delhi was well aware of the type of political fallout that its nuclear test would generate. Shortly afterward, Indian Prime Minister Indira Gandhi wrote a letter to her Pakistani counterpart and assured him that the explosion had no military, political, or foreign policy implications.[46]

The stability and instability of nuclear deterrence between India and Pakistan also has been a major issue of concern since 1980s. Proponents of nuclear deterrence in South Asia who argue that the introduction of the nuclear weapons has prevented the outbreak of a large-scale conflict between India and Pakistan, generally belong to the "State-as-a-rational-actor" school of thought. Other worry about the new threat against the stability of nuclear deterrence in South Asia posed by the intrusion of non state actors, or perhaps, more accurately "anti state actors." Non state or anti state actors have brought nuclear- armed Pakistan and India to the Brink of war, which could have escalated to the nuclear level, twice since 11 September 2001. Despite recent efforts at de-escalation, the danger of war remains high because Islamist militants in Kashmir and elsewhere have the potential and reasons to re-ignite tensions between New Delhi and Islamabad by doing something so outrageous and provocative that India would feel compelled to retaliate.[47]

India and Pakistan's past behavior shows that there is little or no danger of either side firing a nuclear weapon in anger or because of miscalculation. In all three wars, both sides avoided wars of attrition or deliberate targeting of population and industrial centers. The leaders from both capitals insist that nuclear weapons are only for deterrence and are not weapons of war. It is conceivable that Pakistan could use nuclear weapons if faced total defeat by India. Indians argue, however, that they have no interest in destroying the Pakistan state and incorporating another 140 million Muslims into the Indian state. If New Delhi goes for war with Islamabad, the war will be over Kashmir, not the existent of Pakistan. Policymakers in New Delhi and Islamabad have sound understanding of each other's capabilities, intensions, policies and more important red lines which they are careful not to cross. New Delhi and Islamabad believe that nuclear deterrence is working to prevent the war in the region. They point to fact that neither 1999 Kargil conflict nor the post September 11 military standoff escalated beyond a limited conventional engagement due to the threat of nuclear war. So the stability argument based on the reasonable conclusion that nuclear weapons have served an important purpose in the sense that India and Pakistan have not gone to an all out war since 1971. Just as nuclear deterrence maintained stability between United States and USSR during cold war, so it can induce similar stabilizing effects in South Asia.[48]

The preceding analysis of the perspective of anti state actors shows that deterrence in South Asia may not work in the context of asymmetric and unrestricted warfare based on surprise, shock, and deception and waged by those who have little or nothing to lose, particularly when suicide is used as a weapon. The instability argument points to the following reason:[49]

The history of four war; the intensity, duration, and complexity of the animosity; and growing domestic pressure in each country for action against the other make nuclear deterrence unstable. The war on terrorism has encouraged brinkmanship on both sides with both India and Pakistan seeing the US presence in the region as a safety net. The next nuclear confrontation could be even more dangerous if the two sides follow the cold war era, US Soviet standoff model with nuclear missiles on alert, aimed at each other, and ready to launch on warning. As lee Butler former head of the US Strategic Command, has said, it was "no thanks to deterrence, but only by the grace of God" that the US and Soviet Union survived there crises. India and Pakistan may not be lucky the next time.

Whereas the cold war was ideological, the India – Pakistan conflict is historical and religious. More than disputed borders, India – Pakistan share disputed histories. The US and Soviet Union never engaged in direct military conflict with each other. Nor did they have a history of military conflict or animosity prior to the 1940s. Nonetheless they still came close to war more than once.

The sharing of a border and their territorial disputes are rooted in a deep religious divide, going back one thousand years – such as the desire to reestablish Islamic or Hindu supremacy over the entire subcontinent. Indians and Pakistanis have bitter memories of highly emotional issues too long to list: invasions, partition, three wars, religious and border disputes, volatile political cultures, inflammatory media and two decades of low intensity conflict. None of these factors existed as potential fuses to light the nuclear powder keg during the US – Soviet nuclear standoff.

Neither Pakistan nor India Possesses accurate intelligence or warning systems, nor do they have the ability to assure a second strike. The fear of a decisive first strike "use it or lose it" option with short distances, poor warning systems, and small stockpiles amidst the talk of "nuclear jihad" make deterrence very unstable. As a result, the possibility of a nuclear conflict in South Asia, by design or accident, cannot be ruled out entirely because of their (1) week, untested command and control system,(2) relative inexperience in managing nuclear weapons, and (3) lack of knowledge about each other's military processes make it possible to cross a "line in the sand" unintentionally.

In contrast, Pakistan publicly has flexed its nuclear muscles on four occasions in recent history (1987, 1990, 1999 and 2002). India also repeatedly has warned that it would survive a nuclear war, but Pakistan surely would disappear from the world map. (The world has not heard such a threat since the 1950s when Mao Zedong argued that enough Chinese would survive a nuclear confrontation with the United States to usher in a communist revolution.) In short, neither periodic threats of nuclear annihilation nor nuclear blackmail bode well for stable nuclear deterrence.

The freelance factor of terrorism changes the situational context completely in the sense that antistate actors may have vested interest in provoking a war between India and Pakistan. With relatively little radioactive material obtained from low-level waste from a power plant or medical facility, terrorists could easily construct a 'dirty bomb' using simple explosive. Such devices, hidden in a truck or shipborne cargo container headed for Karachi or Bombay, could inflict considerable casualties followed by widespread radiation poisoning.

The China factor further adds to the unpredictability, complexity, and instability of the subcontinental nuclear power balance. China long has been the most important player in the India-Pakistan -China triangular relationship. The Sino-Pakistani military alliance(in particular, the nuclear and missile nexus) is aimed at ensuring that the military balance of power in South Asia is neither pro India nor pro Pakistan but pro china. Most war gaming exercise on the next Indian-Pakistani nuclear war end in Chinese military intervention to prevent the collapse of Beijing's most allied ally in Asia.

Nuclear deterrence works through the minds of not only those who are connected with the two NCAs but also those of the articulate public in two countries. The contest to influence them in strategically favourable ways is just only beginning.

External Environment:

While examining Pakistan's management of its external security environment, the underlying geo-strategic compulsions standout, more so in the light of Freud's saying of "territory being destiny". Pakistan's geography and location present its security planners with serious, almost insoluble strategic and tactical problems. It borders a powerful India, an ambitious Iran, a three decade old strategic ally China, and Afghanistan, which Pakistan has transformed in less than a decade as a client state that is perceived as a gateway to its commercial-strategic ambitions in Central Asia. Besides their obvious repercussions in Central Asia and Afghanistan, these struggles could have potentially spill-over effects on India and China. In the overall geo-economic and strategic configuration, involving west Asia, central Asia, China and Afghanistan, Pakistan will continue to find its relevance to American and Chinese interests in Southern Asia and would increasingly seek to astutely balance India in strategic terms.[50]

China-Pakistan Axis:

In geo-political terms, the decades long convergence of strategic interests between China and Pakistan is inherently India centric with China seeking an added bonus in of a toe –hold in West Asia and possibility of egress into the Arabian Sea through the trans Himalayan road highway.

Their friendship is often described by Pakistanis and Chinese as "Loftier than the Himalayas and deeper than the Indian Ocean". Peculiarities of geography and history have linked the two in the India-China strategic friction and territorial dispute. China would for decades remain India's strategic challenge. Pakistan got from China not only a range of nuclear capable missiles—M-11, M-9, and D-F 21/21A, meant specifically to counter India. Beijing willfully fuelled Pakistan's ambitions to be a regional influential, a development which may one day boomerang on it. By way of a delicious irony, china's intensified support for Pakistan's nuclear- delivery missile programme. Thus when china's bilateral relations with India were thawing makes one inference clear Beijing willfully introduced an adversarial impulse in India-China relations by encouraging and endorsing Pakistan's ambitions to be a regional influential. That means adopted were to equip it with ballistic missiles having ranges well beyond those needed to balance India. From among developing countries, Pakistan economic and military value lies as much in its being the foremost importer of China's nuclear and weapons technology as in its serving as an excellent source of hard currency earnings. These linkages are expected to be sustained over the years. Today about 70 percent of Pakistan's military hardware is of Chinese origin. A trend of significant military consequence to India is that the on-going military modernization in China, including induction of forces multipliers, would provide Pakistan a siphon-off technological benefit through access to these systems apart from Su-27s, MBTs, kilo class submarines and other equipment. Armed with these capabilities and nuclear- tipped Chinese-supplied ballistic missiles, Pakistan may well perceive itself as a lynchpin of China's grand design for South Asian security in 21st century[51].

American Role:

America's role in Pakistan's geopolitical transformation as a regional influential, notwithstanding its extant internal and economic travails, need to be addressed briefly. During the concluding Cold war years, Pakistan was cultivated as a "frontline" state in America's sustained drive to reverse the former Soviet Union influence in Afghanistan. As a quid pro quo, Pakistan's determined and often clandestine attempts to become a nuclear power were conveniently overlooked. These supportive influences largely facilitated Pakistan in acquiring the necessary capabilities from china. Lamentably, the global non-proliferation regime, so assiduously created by the west over the years, has been powerless against China's repeated successes in flouting the same through missile transfers to Pakistan. The United States leadership has consistently chosen to turn a blind eye to such sales even when these transgressed the Missile Technology Control Regime, Sino-American agreements and solemn Chinese promises.

Despite claims to the contrary from both the United States and China, their implicit strategic congruence on the latter's nuclear missile assistance to Pakistan has been palpable. Yet it is ironic that many influential sections in

Pakistan's top leadership, particularly the military elements, do not consider America a trustworthy ally. It would be instructive to recall the mindset of Islamic solidarity that prevailed within the Pakistani leadership just prior to the gulf war in 1991. The anti American perception would appear to have gained further momentum after American attacks on the Saudi fugitive and terrorist leader Osama Bin Laden's camps in Afghanistan. However at the official level, the country's leadership continues to perpetuate the myth of Pakistan being the only reliable bridge between the US and many areas of strategic interest to Washington. During Prime Minister Nawaz Sharif's 1998 meeting with President Clinton at New York, the former has reportedly projected Pakistan as one nation with the ability to defuse the tension between Taliban and Iran. The United state would need to relook at how an unintended consequence of its support to the Taliban could well result in eventual "Talibanisation" of Pakistan itself with deeadful consequences for the region, particularly India. Pakistan should be encouraged to go along with the broad trend in Islamic countries towards moderation and promotion of dialogue between civilizations as part of a cooperative paradigm of security. This would demand Pakistan having to throttle back on its religious extremism driven support for militancy in the region.[52]

Central Asia and Afghanistan:

Notwithstanding Pakistan's endemic internal turbulence, it seems seriously engaged in re-orienting its foreign policy goals to play a wider role. The preoccupation to exploit the central Asian option is self evident, for the United States, the importance of this area of potential strategic advantage, given the vast natural resources and untapped oil and gas in Kazakhstan, Turkmenistan and Uzbekistan, has been extensively documented in the media. Pakistan looks at Central Asian Muslim states as the future arena for its diplomatic and economic initiatives as it can offer these republics the shortest outlet to the sea. Besides, instabilities in the domestic and interstate politics of these countries make it hard for Pakistan to devise a coherent approach. They are also wary of Pakistan's parallel agenda for Islamic resurgence and seem to give the impression of preferring a more moderate line.

Taliban's capture of Mazar-e-Sharif and most of the northern areas and its being in occupation of nearly 85 percent of Afghan territory has doubtless created a new situation. The aggressive Islamic fundamentalist ideology that the Taliban espouses has worrisome implications for Central Asia, India and China. Ever since the Soviet withdrawal in 1989, Islamabad has been unwavering in its resolve to establish a Pakistan dominated government in Kabul that obtaining strategic depth against India. For India, there is the added danger that the Islamic mercenary elements who participated in the Taliban's sweep across Afghanistan may now turn their attention towards India, and particularly the state of J&K. This would place an even greater strain on the Indian Army, paramilitary forces and central police elements who are employed in counter militancy operations. But the regional implications of trans-border Taliban incursions are far more serious and need careful consideration. For India and Pakistan there is a path of peace and cooperation in this 21st century era of compelling change would offer no other alternative.[53]

Confidence-building measure(CBMs):

CBMs are state practices that are intended to increase the level of trust and to lower the likelihood of conflict. It is believed that through communication, constraints, transparency and verification, and CBMs, the behavior of state became more predictable. These measures have usually followed crisis events. These agreements are scattered over the 13 year under consideration and have been concluded by governments articulating both the secular and religious culture national identity[54].

Military CBMs:

India and Pakistan completed the ratification process of Indo-Pak agreements on prohibition of attacks on each other's nuclear installations and facilities in 27 January, 1991. Since then, as stipulated in the agreements, India and Pakistan have exchange list of nuclear installations and facilities every year. This agreement has been undertaken irrespective of the degree of tension prevailing between the two countries. In fact, this stipulation has been met even when diplomatic engagement with Pakistan was severed during the crisis triggered by the events of October and December 2001. However the effectiveness of this agreement remains in doubt since it is not clear whether Islamabad and Delhi have forwarded the complete list of all the nuclear installations in their respective states. This agreement was signed on the basis of the previous talk on advance notice of military exercise and prevention of air space violations. It was decided that India and Pakistan would avoid holding major military manoeuvres in close proximity, and if held, these exercise would not be directed towards the other side. These agreements were ratified in 1992 when Narashimha Rao was the Prime Minister of India. In, fact several other agreements were arrived at as well. These two countries signed a joint declaration on the complete prohibition chemical weapons, and agreed that Directors General Military Operations(DGMO) of the two countries should speak to each other every week on a hotline.[55]

In 1994 India proposed the following CBMs: extending the agreement on prohibition of attacks on nuclear installations to population center and economic targets; no first use of nuclear weapons are even the threat of it; upgrading links between DGMOs; and setting up of institutional mechanism to implement agreements arrived at. It was the Lahore agreement that the issue of military CBMs was raised again. In fact soon after the test in May 1998, India and Pakistan held foreign secretary level meetings in June and November of the same year. No doubt these were also the result of intense international pressure. Eventually, at Lahore, the MoU signed by the foreign secretaries on 21 February 1999, stipulated that 'the two sides shall engage in bilateral consultations on security concept and nuclear doctrines.[56] It was agreed that two states would provide advance notification of ballistic missile tests, seek to prevent accidents at sea, review implementation of previous CBMs and improve communication links but after these talks the two countries agreed to have a structured procedure.[57] Both states are acknowledge to be nuclear weapons sates though outside the ambit of the Non-Proliferation Treaty(NPT), Even while the capabilities remain in a state of non-deployed, non-weaonized states, CBMs are expected to 'Contribute to generating an atmosphere of thrust and mutual understanding between the two countries. This is a new mindset and it reflected in the two sides.[58]

Non-Military CBMs:

Essentially, these are the agreements and gestures that are intended to soften friction and tension prevalent between states, to increase trust and provide an atmosphere conductive for serious dialog. For instance, oftentimes the discussions between foreign secretaries or the heads of state were preceded by goodwill gesture that involved either easing of visa process or the release of fishermen captured at sea. In Lahore declaration, both sides agreed to resolve all issues including Kashmir, refrained from interference in each other's affair, intensify their composite dialogue process, combat terrorism in all its forms and manifestations, and take immediate step for reducing the risk of accidental or unauthorized nuclear weapons. Further, after Kargil India proposed a series of CBMs such as 20 scholarships and student visas to Pakistani students to study at India's top technical institutions, a meeting of DGMOs, unilateral tariff concesions on 50 items and visa relaxations. These proposals were dismissed by Musharraf, who stated that the only CBM was the resolution of Kashmir. The next round of CBMs was proposed in October 2003. Effort towards normalization of relations had begun as early as spring 2003 after Vajpayee called for another attempt to resolve differences. This resulted in a series of back- channel discussions between Brajesh Mishra(India's NSA) and Tariq Aziz(Musharraf's confidante). In India, the gradual easing of tension was the subject of considerable debate amongst the members of the Congress Party who questioned the judgment of the government in resuming relations even as there was no significant end to cross-border terrorism. In response, Vajpayee stated:

"As a neighbor and with a neighbor, we have to live with a feeling of friendship.... However it is, if there is no opportunity to have good relations, it should not be lost?... we can chang friends but we cannot change neighbours. Neither can they go somewhere nor can we. Now one route is that we be friends as neighbours.... Or we keep fighting."

This speech echoes the sentiments of Narshima Rao when he was Prime Minister of India. Commenting on Indo-Pak relations, Rao had observed in 1991, 'where do we stand? We stand exactly where we stood always. We have to ready for any eventuality but at the same time, we have to persist in our efforts to improve relations to the extent we can. Later in 1994 he stated that India had to learn to live with Pakistan[59].

In 2005 the two sides envisage turning the LoC into a soft border with more bus services as also opening it for trade.[60] Besides, both states have opened the Attari Border for the transportation of goods through trucks and considered working for joint disaster management techniques in case of eventualities. During the earth quake in October 2005 India not only send a relief of 112 Crores but also opend its LoC at five places: Rawalkot-Poonch, Kamon-Chakoti, Teetwal-Nauseri, Mandhar-Tatta Pani and Sialkot-Haji Peer.[61] India thus proposed the following measures: technical discussions for resumption of civil aviation(especially over flights), Discussions for rail links and air links , bilateral sporting events, visa camps, border crossing by senior citizens(at Wagah checkpoint and by foot), capacity increases on Delhi-Lahor bus service, links between the two coast guards, agreement to not arrest fishermen in certain areas, free medical treatment to 20 Pakistani children, ferry service between Mumbai and Karachi, frequency of bus service between Srinagar and Muzaffarabad should be increased from fortnightly to a weekly basis and should be start between Khokrapar(Pakistan's Sindh province) and Munabao (India's Rajasthan state)[62]. While Pakistan accepted some of the CBMs, it rejected others such as bus links between towns in JK and Sind or the ferry service between Karachi and Mumbai. In case of the bus service between Srinagar and Muzaffarabad, it was proposed that UN officials man checkpoints and that people travel with UN documents. This was unacceptable to the Indian government, which has been extremely wary of international presence along the LoC. Pakistan also proposed a bus link between Lahore and Amritsar, which the Indian government said it would consider. Pakistan further sought the restoration of its full diplomatic staff in India and offered 100 scholarships to the people from JK and free treatment to disabled, widows and victims of rape. In its response to Pakistani proposals, India rejected the discriminatory focus on JK, arguing that India had never adopted a selective approach for the regions within Pakistan and that if Pakistan was concerned about the plight of Kashmiris, it should end cross-border terrorism[63]. The Pakistani delegation did not agree to the Indian proposal of a series of CBMs which covered exchanges like holding seminars academics and research institutions dealing with strategic and defence related issues. The Indian proposal also called for exchanges, lectures, seminars between the defence training establishments like National Defence Colleges.[64]

Footnote

1. B.J.C. Mckercher(ed.), Routledge Handbook of Diplomacy and Statecraft, Routledge, London, 2012, p.402.
2. Donette Murray and David Brown(eds.), Multipolarity in 21st Century, A new world order, Routledge, London, 2012, p. 141.
3. C. Raja Mohan, "How Obama Can Get South Asia Right" The Washigaton Quarterly, vol.32, no.2, April, 2009, p.175.
4. Saeed Ahmeh Rid, "Kashmir: the Prisoner's Dilemma for India and Pakistan", South Asian Journal of Peacebuilding, vol.4,no.2, Winter 2012, pp.2-3.
5. Bhumitra Chakma, "Road to Chagai: Pakistan's Nuclear Programme, Its Sources and Motivations", Modern Asian Studies, Vol.36, no.4, October, 2002, p.903.

6. Bhumitra Chakma, "Road to Chagai: Pakistan's Nuclear Programme, Its Sources and Motivations", Modern Asian Studies, Vol.36, no.4, October, 2002, p.904.
7. Mohan Malik, "The Stability of Nuclear Deterrence in South Asia: The Clash between State and Antistate Actors", Asian Affairs, Vol.30, no.3, 2003, pp. 187-190.
8. Ashok K. Behuria, "Pakistan's Apporach to Kashmir Since the Lahore Agreement: Is there Any Change?", Strategic Analysis, vol.33, no.3, May 2009, p.434.
9. Gurmeet Kanwal, "Pakistan's Strategic Blunder in Kargil", Strategic Analysis, vol. 23, no.5, August, 1999, pp. 838-840.
10. "India and Pakistan survey", The Economist, May 22, 1999, p.17.
11. Saeed Ahmeh Rid, "Kashmir: the Prisoner's Dilemma for India and Pakistan", South Asian Journal of Peacebuilding, vol.4,no.2, Winter 2012, pp.2-3.
12. ---------
13. C. Raja Mohan, "How Obama Can Get South Asia Right" The Washigaton Quarterly, vol.32, no.2, April, 2009, p.176.
14. John Briscoe, "Troubled Waters: Can a Bridge be Built over the Indus?", Economic & Political Weekly, Vol. 45, no.50, December 11, 2010, p.28.
15. Neeru Sharma, "Indus Water Treaty(IWT) and Water, Conflicts Between India and Pakistan", Punjab Journal of Politics, Vol. 30, no.2, 2006, p.5.
16. John Briscoe, "Troubled Waters: Can a Bridge be Built over the Indus?", Economic & Political Weekly, Vol. 45, no.50, December 11, 2010, p.29.
17. Ramaswamy R Iyer, "Briscoe on the Indus Treaty: A Response", Economic & Political Weekly, vol.46, no.3, January 15, 2011, p.69.
18. Ibid, p.69.
19. Ashutosh Misra, "An audit of India-Pakistan peace process" Australian Journal of International Affairs, Vol. 61, no.4, December, 2007, p.514.
20. Satyabrat Sinha, "The India-Pakistan Peace Process: Incremental Progress?", in Anjali Ghosh and others(ed.), India's foreign Policy, New Delhi,2009,p.233.
21. Iftikar Gialni, "India Considering Siachen Proposal", at http://www.dailytimes.com.pk.
22. Syed Imran Sardar, "Conflict Transformation: A Paradigm Shift in Indo-Pakistan Conflict", Regional Studies, vol.29, no.2, Spring 2011, p.28.
23. Ashutosh Misra, "An audit of India-Pakistan peace process" Australian Journal of International Affairs, Vol. 61, no.4, December, 2007, p.514.
24. Joint Press Statement on India-Pakistan Talk on Sir Creek, New Delhi, 7 August, 2004, at http://meaindia.nic.in.

25. Iftikhar A. Khan, "Sir Creek Differences Remain", 19, May 2007, at http://www.dawn.com.

26. M Kreopn and A Sevak(eds), Crisis Prevention, Confidence Building and Reconciliation in South Asia, St. Martin's Press, New York, 1995, p.95.

27. Ashutosh Misra, "An audit of India-Pakistan peace process" Australian Journal of International Affairs, Vol. 61, no.4, December, 2007, p.519.

28. Rajen Harshe, "Cross Border Terrorism, Road Block to Peace Initiatives", Economic and Political Weekly, vol. 38, no. 35, August 30, 2003, p. 3622.

29. Matthew Rosenstein, "Editorial", Defense & Security Analysis, vol.22, no.4, December 2006, p.345.

30. Priyanka Singh, "Militant Training Camps in Pakistan – Occupied Kashmir: An Existential Threat", Strategic Analysis, vol. 33, no. 3, May, 2009, p. 334.

31. Teresita C. Schaffer and Howard B. Schaffer, "India and Pakistan: A Time of Uncertainty" Trip report, January,27- February 15, 2009, pp.1-2.

32. Talat Ayesha Wizarat, "Transformation of State Borders: Implications for Pakistan", Regional Studies, vol.29, Summer, 2011, p.15.

33. Rajen Harshe, "Cross Border Terrorism, Road Block to Peace Initiatives", Economic and Political Weekly, vol. 38, no. 35, August 30, 2003, p. 3622.

34. Zahid Ali Khan Marwat, "Indian and Pakistani Missile Programmes: A Comparative Study", Regional Studies, vol.19, no.2, Spring, 2011, p.93.

35. Zahid Ali Khan Marwat, "Indian and Pakistani Missile Programmes: A Comparative Study", Regional Studies, vol.19, no.2, Spring, 2011, p.93.

36. Zahid Ali Khan Marwat, "Indian and Pakistani Missile Programmes: A Comparative Study", Regional Studies, vol.19, no.2, Spring, 2011, p.93

37. Anupam Srivastava, " Strategic Import of Missile in the Indian Security Policy: Can they Deliver the Goods", at www.rediffonthent.com, August, 2009.

38. Monika Chansoria, "India Missile Programme: Augmenting the firepower", at http://www.drdo.org, October 2009.

39. "PJ-10 BrahMos", at http://www.global-security.org.

40. "DRDO to Devlop Long Range, Subsonic Cruise Missile", India Defencea, 21, October, 2007, at http://www.india.defance.com.

41. "Pakistan derives its first 'Hatf' missile from foreign space rocket", The Risk Report, Vol.1, no.8, October, 1995, at http://www.wisconsinproject.org.

42. Zahid Ali Khan Marwat, "Indian and Pakistani Missile Programmes: A Comparative Study", Regional Studies, vol.19, no.2, Spring, 2011, p.107.

43. Zahid Ali Khan Marwat, "Indian and Pakistani Missile Programmes: A Comparative Study", Regional Studies, vol.19, no.2, Spring, 2011, p.108.

44. http://www.app.com.
45. S.M. Hali, "Ra,ad Roars", The Nations, Islamabad, 29 August, 2007, at http://www.thenations.com .
46. Verghese Koithara, "Coercion and Risk-Talking in Nuclear South Asia" CISAC Working Paper, March, 2003, p.16.
47. Bhumitra Chakma, "Road to Chagai: Pakistan's Nuclear Programme, Its Sources and Motivations", Modern Asian Studies, Vol.36, no.4, October, 2002, p.887-888.
48. Mohan Malik, "The Stability of Nuclear Deterrence in South Asia: The Clash between State and Antistate Actors", Asian Affairs, Vol.30, no.3, 2003, pp. 177-178.
49. Mohan Malik, "The Stability of Nuclear Deterrence in South Asia: The Clash between State and Antistate Actors", Asian Affairs, Vol.30, no.3, 2003, pp. 184-185.
50. Mohan Malik, "The Stability of Nuclear Deterrence in South Asia: The Clash between State and Antistate Actors", Asian Affairs, Vol.30, no.3, 2003, pp. 191-195.
51. Kapil Kak, " Pakistan: A Geo-Political Appriaisal", Strategic Analysis, vol.22, n.8, November 1998, p.1131.
52. Kapil Kak, " Pakistan: A Geo-Political Appriaisal", Strategic Analysis, vol.22, n.8, November 1998, p.1133.
53. Kapil Kak, " Pakistan: A Geo-Political Appriaisal", Strategic Analysis, vol.22, n.8, November 1998, p.1135.
54. Kapil Kak, " Pakistan: A Geo-Political Appriaisal", Strategic Analysis, vol.22, n.8, November 1998, p.1137.
55. Gitika Commuri, Indian Identity Narratives and the Politics of Security, Sage Publication, New Delhi, 2010, p.202.
56. Gitika Commuri, Indian Identity Narratives and the Politics of Security, Sage Publication, New Delhi, 2010, p.203.
57. Gitika Commuri, Indian Identity Narratives and the Politics of Security, Sage Publication, New Delhi, 2010, pp. 203-204.
58. Amit Mishra, "Foreign Minister Meeting", 2-6, October, 2005, Indo- Pak Peace Process Update no.10 at http://ipcs.org.
59. Siddharth Varadarajan, "It's Time for Boldness on Siachen Issue", The Hindu, 14, September, 2005.
60. Gitika Commuri, Indian Identity Narratives and the Politics of Security, Sage Publication, New Delhi, 2010, p.210.
61. Anjli Ghosh and Others(eds), India's Foreign Policy, New Delhi, Pearson, 2009, p.237.

62. R.S. Yadav, "India-Pakistan Peace Process: A Study of CBMs", South Asian Studies, vol.43, no.1, January-December, 2008, p.93.
63. Hernaikh Singh and Tridivesh Singh Mani, South Asia in 2008 A Review, Manohar Publication, New Delhi, 2009, p.414.
64. Gitika Commuri, Indian Identity Narratives and the Politics of Security, Sage Publication, New Delhi, 2010, p.211.
65. Press Briefings, On Second round of Expert Level Talks Between India and Pakistan on conventional CBMs at http://www.mea.gov.in.

4

Economic and Trade Challenges and India Pakistan Relations

Economic Relations:

In recent months India and Pakistan have unveiled a number of unprecedented trade and commerce initiatives aimed at normalization of bilateral economic relations. The two countries now seem to be at a point where both understand the importance of economic engagement as a means to improve peace prospects. The announcement by the Indian Government on August 1, 2012, to allow Foreign Direct Investment (FDI) from Pakistan has given yet another fillip to Indo-Pak economic relations in the somewhat uncertain environment that was beginning to emerge. There are still some unanswered questions, but once addressed India and Pakistan would have covered yet another milestone in their journey towards normalizing trade and economic relations. Until recently, India had Sri Lanka, Bangladesh and Pakistan on the negative list; however in 2006 and 2007, India permitted FDI from Sri Lanka and Bangladesh respectively, making Pakistan the only country from where India did not permit any FDI inflows. The recent announcement to allow FDI from Pakistan marks a significant change on two counts. First, India no longer has any country on its negative list of foreign investors in its FDI policy. Secondly, the announcement has restored confidence among those who perceived a slowdown in the momentum of normalizing the economic relationship between the two countries following a series of events starting May 2012. This included the postponement of the liberalization of the visa regime between India and Pakistan and the delay in following up on India's Commerce Minister Anand Sharma's promise in April this year to allow FDI from Pakistan.

Another dampening factor was the "inconclusiveness" of energy talks that the two countries had started in March this year. Trade in energy can bring about a quantum jump in India-Pakistan trade. The opening of a US$ 4 billion plant in April 2012 on the northern border with Pakistan at Bhatinda by Mittal Energy Investments and Hindustan Petroleum was expected to gain significantly from the energy talks. The slowdown in the process of strengthening trade and economic relations between the two countries was reversed on August 1, 2012 when India's Department of Industrial Policy and Promotion (DIPP) notified changes in the consolidated FDI policy to allow investment from Pakistan in sectors/activities apart from defence, space and atomic energy through government route and made the requisite amendment. Following this, India recently removed Pakistan from the negative list under the Foreign Exchange Management Act, paving the way for investment from Pakistan. Even in the case of outward FDI flows from India to Pakistan, the FEMA regulations had been an inhibiting factor. Pakistan, on the other hand, has maintained a liberal investment policy with no restrictions on inward investment from, and outward investment, to India. In this context the circular issued by the Reserve Bank of India (RBI) allowing Indians to invest overseas in Pakistan under the "government" route is an important confidence building move. This opening up of investment opportunities has been hailed by businesses on both sides and will likely open up other multi-dimensional opportunities. There is no doubt that encouraging two-way investments will enhance business confidence on both sides. An enabling business environment between the two countries will promote joint ventures and allow firms to access technologies, which in turn will lead to productivity improvement, generating growth and employment opportunities. The private sector is expected to step in to assess bilateral investment possibilities.

Though at the moment it appears that investment possibilities for Pakistani investors are limited. If we look at the year 2011, Pakistan's total outward FDI flow was only US$ 62 million while India's was US$ 14.8 billion. Further, Pakistan's inward FDI flow for 2011 was US$1.3 billion while that of India was US$31.6 billion. The chambers of commerce in the two countries have identified clothing, clothing accessories, fabric, surgical instruments, and cutlery as some of the possible sectors for Pakistani investment. There are larger possibilities for Indian investors in Pakistan in sectors such as chemicals, pharmaceuticals, automobile components, and information technology. In the seventh round of talks on Commercial and Economic Co-operation held in Islamabad between the commerce secretaries of India and Pakistan on September 20-21, 2012, the Pakistani side recognized efforts by India to remove restrictions on inbound and outbound investment to Pakistan. However, they raised concerns about the "government" route and its implications for Pakistani investors in India.

Under India's FDI policy, an Indian company can receive foreign direct investment under two routes – automatic route and government route. According to the RBI guidelines, under the automatic route, investors do not require any prior approval from either the government or the Reserve Bank of India. On the other hand, under the government route, investors require prior approval from the Foreign Investment Promotion Board (FIPB), Department of Economic Affairs, Ministry of Finance. The FIPB is the government body that provides a single window clearance for foreign investment proposals into the country that are not permitted via the automatic route. This agency discusses and examines proposals for investments in sectors that are not allowed via the automatic route under FDI policy. For investors from Pakistan and Bangladesh, the "government route" applies to all sectors. The investors from these countries are concerned on two fronts – transparency and time taken for approvals. However, it needs to be noted in India an e-filing facility was introduced in March 2012 to enhance the efficiency and transparency of decision-making under the government route. Under this facility, investors can apply for approvals directly and complete applications filed three weeks prior to a scheduled FIPB meeting are taken up for consideration. The FIPB meetings are held on a regular basis, usually once in 4-5 weeks, to clear applications. The committee declares the approved cases, deferred cases, and the cases that have been rejected. It also provides comments to enable investors to revise and resubmit their applications. These decisions are publicly available on the FIPB website. These systems in place for investments under the government route will enable the two countries to assess the status of applications made by Pakistani investors on a regular basis.

The next step for the governments of India and Pakistan should be to set up an institutional mechanism that would guarantee each other's investments. The countries should work towards signing a bilateral investment treaty that protects and promotes investments of investors on a reciprocal basis and includes provisions on fair and equitable treatment, protection from expropriation and national treatment. Another important issue that needs to be addressed in facilitating bilateral trade and investment between the two countries is allowing banking operations on a reciprocal basis. This would also promote further economic interaction. Action on this front has already been initiated with the commencement of talks between the Reserve Bank of India and the State Bank of Pakistan earlier this year. As India moves towards completing the important task of liberalizing investment flows, it will reinforce its commitment to the trade and investment agenda laid down by the two countries in April 2011. Stronger and deeper economic ties will not only benefit the two countries, but will also serve as a powerful means of confidence building and, in time, of peaceful bilateral relations.[1] Like many other developing countries, South Asian nations have been experiencing increased FDI inflows over the past decade. Compared to total inflows, intra-regional flows of FDI seem to be increasing, but still accounted for only about 5 percent of total cumulative FDI in the past three decades. India accounts for over 90 percent of these FDI flows in South Asia.

Prospects for Indian Investment in Pakistan

Pakistan's geographical location, liberal foreign investment policy, conducive business environment, and a young skilled workforce make it an investor-friendly destination. Strategically located in South Asia, Pakistan is at the crossroads of China, the Central Asian Republics (CAR), and the Gulf States. Pakistan's large market offers huge opportunities to investors from India in terms of the easy access it can provide to markets in Iran, Afghanistan, the Middle East, and CAR. Pakistan's foreign investment policy has been designed as a comprehensive framework to create a conducive business environment to attract FDI. The investment policy offers foreign investors several incentives with respect to tax and to regulations on repatriation of capital and profit. Pakistan has enacted the Law of Special Economic Zones[2] that allows the creation of industrial clusters and offers liberal incentives, infrastructure, and investor facilitation services to enhance productivity and reduce the cost of doing business. An added advantage is its large trained and skilled English-speaking labor force. The consumer market in Pakistan is also growing at a rapid pace and the potential to tap market opportunities provides strong grounds for FDI flows from India into Pakistan.

Indian investment in Pakistan can benefit from several country-specific advantages. The common culture and language between the two countries can immensely facilitate business cooperation. The language spoken is the same in the two Punjabs in the two main cities of the two countries,

Karachi and Mumbai, Sindhi is spoken. There is a certain sense of connect with people across the border. Smooth communication channels help in business interactions by reducing entry and transaction costs. Given the enormous benefits of FDI, increased investment flows between India and Pakistan could be mutually beneficial for both countries. However, the benefits of FDI seem to be larger for Pakistan than for India. A liberal investment regime for FDI flows from India will enable Pakistan to tap into the pool of Indian skilled workers and technology to improve international competitiveness of Pakistani firms.[3] Also, increased investment can boost Pakistan's economic growth and help it overcome the domestic challenges its economy faces. Overall, an improvement in the FDI scenario between India and Pakistan will help strengthen bilateral ties. Against the background of prospects for Indian investment in Pakistan, the following sub-sections analyze the growing importance of India as an overseas investor and Pakistan as an investment destination.

Potential Areas for Indian Investment in Pakistan

As India and Pakistan compete to sell their products in the international market, there are areas in which the two countries can complement each other's needs. There is general interest among businessmen on both sides to invest in the other's country. There is greater interest from the Pakistan side to invest in India in sectors such as cement, hotels, and textiles. There is a general expression of interest by large Indian business houses such as the Tatas and Godrej to invest in Pakistan. Companies such as Dabur already operate via Dubai to cater to the Pakistani market. In September 2013, the first India-Pakistan joint venture took place. A furniture-making firm in Lahore, IWM (Interwood Mobel) Private Ltd.[4] and Noble Trans-links Private Ltd. of Amritsar jointly set up a firm called IWM Interwood Mobel Private Ltd. The stage has been set for investment by these two companies and this precedent should be followed with more such investments. During the course of our industry consultations, interaction with policymakers, and review of research reports, we identified sectors for possible collaboration within three broad categories.

Primary Sector

India and Pakistan are both principally agrarian economies with agriculture contributing 13.7 percent and 21.4 percent to GDP, respectively, in the two countries in 2012–13.[5] Agriculture, with its allied sectors, is unquestionably the largest livelihood provider in both countries. Most industries also depend on this sector for their raw materials. There are considerable opportunities for investment in agriculture and processed foods. Within agriculture, there is tremendous scope for investments/joint ventures in inputs such as seeds, agricultural equipment, and technology.[6] Further, the mining sector offers scope for investment. Based on available information, more than 6,00,000 sq. km of outcrop potentially holds metallic/non-metallic mineral deposits in Pakistan. Except for oil, gas, and nuclear minerals regulated at the federal level, minerals are regulated at the provincial level. The Federal and Provincial governments jointly set out Pakistan's Mineral Policy in 1995, providing the appropriate institutional and regulatory framework and an equitable and internationally competitive fiscal framework. The enforcement of the Mineral Policy has paved the way to expand mining sector activities and attract international investment in this sector. Although the opportunity for Indian investment in the mining and mineral sector is good, past experience may deter investors from investing here. In December 2009, the authorities in Balochistan Province passed a motion and threatened to terminate the exploration mining license of the Reko Diq copper and gold mine held by Canadian Barrick Gold Corporation and a Chilean copper mining company. The threat to cancel the license was reportedly on the grounds that the mining lease application was incomplete and not legally compliant with mining laws.[7] However the Balochistan government called the move a step towards getting control over provincial resources. Despite timely intervention by Pakistan's federal government, the dispute sends a negative image of the otherwise lucrative and welcoming attitude of the government toward FDI and may deter Indian investment in this sector.[8]

Secondary Sector

Pharmaceuticals, textiles, transport, and energy are a few sectors that offer investment potential to Indian investors in the secondary sector. In the pharmaceuticals sector, there is scope for collaboration in bulk drugs and expansion of formulation and health products. Indian pharmaceutical products are cheaper than Pakistani pharmaceutical products and Pakistan's pharmaceutical regime is not strictly regulated for domestic production. There is scope for setting up JVs in Pakistan for sharing technical know-how in this sector. The Indian pharmaceutical industry can provide the necessary support and assistance to Pakistan to expand its industry. Further, this will have a positive impact on Pakistan's industrial growth and help meet the challenge of providing cheaper drugs to Pakistani citizens. The major Indian pharmaceutical player, Biocon, has granted an exclusive license to enter the Pakistan market through a licensing arrangement with Ferozsons Laboratories, Pakistan.[9] There is scope for further FDI in the pharmaceutical sector.

With energy demand rising in Pakistan, the greatest benefit could accrue in the sphere of energy cooperation, which could act as the single most effective confidence building measure. It could result in wider participation from stakeholders and promote market integration in energy-related trade. Several projects involving cross-border trade in coal, hydroelectric power, petroleum products, thermal energy, renewable energy, and bilateral and regional grid interconnection have the potential to be economically viable[10]. Cross-border "power trade" could be done via bilateral power trade, pool-based exchange, or a wheeling facility. Overall, there is high potential for energy trade between the two countries, for which talks are ongoing.[11] India and Pakistan are considering the option of electricity trading. The first meeting of the Joint Group of Experts to examine the feasibility of trade in electricity was held on October 20, 2011 at New Delhi. The Central Electricity Authority and Power Grid Corporation of India Limited/ Power System Operation Corporation Ltd were designated as the nodal technical agencies from the Indian side. They are interacting with the National Transmission and Dispatch Company Ltd. of Pakistan to work out optimal technical solutions for grid connectivity between the two countries. A broad understanding has been reached on possible grid connectivity between Amritsar and Lahore to enable trade of up to 500 MW of power. As of January 2014, the Federal Cabinet in Pakistan approved the signing of a Memorandum of Understanding between the two countries.[12] Given the importance of electricity for Pakistan's domestic economy, the electricity sector can be seen as one of the most important sectors for investment.

Pakistan has been trying to make the energy sector lucrative for Indian investors by offering incentives such as customs and sales tax exemption in Special Economic Zones, zero import duty on machinery for energy plants, etc. There is a need to pass this information to Indian investors. India is one of the most rapidly growing energy markets in the world and will be able to absorb new sources of supply as they materialize in the region. Pakistan can be a potential transit route for energy from Iran and Central Asia through the construction of pipelines. This will require major capital investment. The Iran-Pakistan-India (IPI) pipeline and the

Turkmenistan-Afghanistan-Pakistan-India (TAPI) pipeline are two such ambitious projects, for which negotiations are underway. A huge transit fee and a share in gas supply on a daily basis is the direct benefit that will accrue to Pakistan in such cases.

Energy cooperation between India and Pakistan would have an overall stabilizing effect on the region, and such ventures can be explored in other areas of energy. For example, India can invest in Pakistan's power sector, on which the backbone of the economy—the textile sector—is also dependent. Pakistan experiences major power cuts that adversely affect its industries. FDI in this sector will have twin benefits. First, it will rectify power problems in the domestic economy. Second, it will contribute to attracting more MNCs to Pakistan. Further, investment in such crucial sectors can ensure better safety of investment and promote economic development in the country. For the long-term strategic benefit of the country, proposals for acquisition of overseas assets in the energy sector through PSUs or a special purpose fund are being discussed.

Textile is one sector in which Pakistan has a comparative advantage. However, the textiles sector in Pakistan is not technologically advanced. There is a case for India and Pakistan to leverage each other's comparative advantage by complementing each other. Initially, the opening of trade with India can help Pakistan acquire high-tech machinery at lower prices than the ones it currently acquires from Germany. Further, JVs can help combine the strengths of Pakistan's designs and fabric with Indian marketing skills. This sector offers scope for technology sharing. Pakistan and India are competing for the same international markets. The two countries can jointly cater to international markets, such as Europe, by producing high-quality and cost-effective textile products. In other words, instead of acting as competitors, both countries can collaborate by focusing on value addition and joint marketing for European and ASEAN countries.

Pakistan's performance on most logistics indicators, including quality of trade and transport infrastructure, is lower than for most Asian countries, particularly India.[13] The transport sector in Pakistan suffers from low quality, long travel times, and poor reliability that hinder the economic growth of the country. In this regard, India can offer logistics support to meet increased transportation requirements in Pakistan. India can invest in infrastructure projects similar to its successful home projects like the Delhi Metro. Investments in trade corridors should also be encouraged.

Tertiary Sector

India has established itself as a major player in the Information Technology (IT) segment. Although the software industry in Pakistan is still in its nascent stages, it has the potential to emerge as a major software export and training center. India and Pakistan could enter into joint ventures to tap the global market for software. While Pakistan can provide professionals at lower wages, Indian companies could help procure international contracts.[14] India has a comparative advantage in IT in terms of low-cost, qualified, English-speaking personnel. This can be replicated in Pakistan. Another area where the two countries could gain is if India sets up training institutes in Pakistan or if professionals from Pakistan are allowed to go to India to get professional training. Healthcare services are another area in which there are opportunities for both countries. Owing to relatively efficient health system, India has emerged as an important destination for provision of medical services due to affordable treatment costs and advances in medicine. Despite a relatively tight visa regime, the number of patients going from Pakistan to India has been on the rise. According to a report, the Indian High Commission in Islamabad issued 1,992 medical visas to Pakistani citizens during 2008-10. In addition, 2,917 visas were issued to medical attendants during the same period.[15] Several Pakistani patients have been visiting India for medical treatment, such as liver and kidney transplants and open heart surgery[16] and the Mumbai Obstetric and Gynecological Society provides fertility treatment to Pakistani couples. In April 2014, Indraprastha Apollo Hospitals created a milestone by becoming the first hospital in India to reach the 500th mark for patients from a single foreign country, Pakistan. Patients from Pakistan constitute 29 percent of liver transplants performed at Apollo hospitals, New Delhi. This opens up avenues for further promoting medical tourism between India and Pakistan.

Cross-border investment in hospitals is another potential area of cooperation. Several leading Indian hospitals have entered other markets in the South Asian region through joint ventures with a local partner, wholly owned subsidiaries, or management contracts. There are also tale-medicine links between major hospitals in India and establishments in other South Asian countries, mainly for tale-consultation and tale-diagnostic services. There is no reason as to why branches or subsidiary hospitals cannot be set up in Pakistan as they have done in other South Asian neighbors.[17] For the potential investments to fructify, the two countries have to take measures in several areas. It is important to examine the regulatory regime governing investment flows between India and Pakistan, the existing barriers to investment in Pakistan, and the need for banking channels to facilitate investment flows between the two countries.

Existing Barriers in Pakistan

Despite the investor-friendly nature of the FDI policy offered by Pakistan government, investment from India has not yet entered the Pakistan market. There are tangible and intangible barriers to investing in Pakistan that are not due to the policies, but to the underlying nature of the Pakistan economy. The major barriers in the way of foreign investment are described below.

Law and Order

In recent years, the law and order situation has deteriorated all over the country. It is far from satisfactory even in the growth capital of the country, i.e., Karachi.

Lack of political stability

Political risks largely depend on political stability and governance by the government. Political stability is extremely important for the normal macroeconomic and business environment of a country. It enhances the probability of attracting FDI inflows into countries, as it builds confidence among investors. Several studies show that the degree of political stability is an important factor that investors consider when entering business and it significantly affects FDI flows. If the country's political stability is low, foreign investors hesitate to bring in projects until they are assured that the business environment is conducive and favorable.[18] Pakistan has been suffering from instability in its political system and this can be identified as the most important barrier that has prevented Pakistan from receiving large inflows of FDI from countries including India. Even the World Bank (2011) categorically states that private sector investment is low in the country because of political instability and corruption.

Since 2008, political instability in the country has increased. One measure of political instability is the political instability index that shows the level of threat posed to governments by social protest.

Pakistan's FDI in India: Potential and Prospects

The recent announcement by the Indian Government regarding opening up of the country's Foreign Direct Investment (FDI) regime for Pakistani investors comes at a time when India- Pakistan trade normalization process is progressing at an encouraging pace. It is no surprise that investors from both countries have been working closely in joint ventures in third countries, but have not been able to progress in terms of bilateral investments because of political barriers. However, there were some who managed to bypass such barriers; more recently, Pakistani businessmen based and registered in places like Dubai and Malaysia have started investing in India through partnership agreements with Indian resident businessmen. Investors on both sides are ready to employ competitive advantages in their neighborhood and reap economies of scale. The examples of India's Tata group showing interest in Pakistan's energy sector and Pakistan's Mansha group showing interest in India's banking sector show that, on both sides, the business community has done its homework towards exploring its niches. Academia and development partners have long demonstrated through empirical methods how supply chain development in South Asian countries can benefit the region as a whole. Sadly, not much research exists specifically for India and Pakistan at the sectoral level. However, the recent experience of Pakistani investors in Bangladesh proves the win-win case that will be possible for India and Pakistan. Around 2008, several Pakistani textile firms opened branches in Bangladesh to reap the benefits of Least Developed Country (LDC) status, which allows Bangladesh duty free access or reduced tariffs in foreign markets, particularly the EU and US, where major market exists for Pakistan's readymade garments. During 2010 on Pakistani firms that opened branches in Bangladesh show employment creation for Bangladesh's labor force, technology transfer for Bangladesh's textile sector,

increased royalty for Pakistani investors and increased exports of raw material to Bangladesh. A similar story has been observed in the case of Pakistan's investments in Sri Lanka in sectors such as food processing and construction materials. Replicating the regional experiences for India-Pakistan should not be difficult given the sheer size of the two economies and the opportunity presented by a large – and growing – domestic demand in both countries. While Pakistan is soon expected to reciprocate India's decision to open up FDI, several complementary reforms may also be required to ensure smooth flow of investments between the two countries. First, the home departments on both sides should ensure that the recently agreed visa liberalization policy between the two countries is implemented fully and expanded to other cities on an expedient basis. Allowing physical capital to move while human capital is curtailed does more harm to the production process, and prevents future cash flows. This happened last year when Pakistan's government drastically reduced the sensitive list and liberalized trade with India. While this allowed steel manufacturers in Pakistan to import machinery at much reduced rates from India in comparison to other parts of the world, such machinery has been lying redundant for weeks, sometimes months, because of delays in allowing visas for Indian engineers who were to come to Pakistan to install the machinery. Second, there is a need to harmonize product standards with the rest of the world. For example, in a discussion with auto part manufacturers in Pakistan it was pointed out that while they were interested in investing in this sector in India, the two industry standards followed by India – Bharat 1 and Bharat 2 – are seen in no other country in the world. Such standards act as barriers to entry for producers who can genuinely enhance consumer surplus in India. The consumer rights organizations in both countries should take note of standards that curtail trade and investment, leading to a decrease in consumer welfare. Third, a natural path in the economic integration for both countries should be to move towards a bilateral investment treaty. This will boost both the safety of investments and boost investor confidence. Under such a treaty, investment from the other country should be treated on par with domestic investors. Similarly, country-specific bias in competition policy and other sector-specific policies needs to be removed. Such treaties allow transfer of investment-related funds into and out of a host country without any delay at the open market exchange rate. Fourth, and a point related to the above, is the need for a sovereign guarantees framework, at least in the short term. Most investors we have come across in Pakistan were fearful that future political friction between the two countries could affect their business in India. It is need to provide sovereign guarantees to investors from Pakistan that ensure full compensation if harm is caused to their investment in India (or Pakistan) due to actions related to foreign or defense policy. It is important to note that such a measure would be unnecessary if the two countries move towards a comprehensive bilateral investment treaty.[19]

Trade between India and Pakistan:

Contiguous countries around the world share a congenial trading environment, with high values of bilateral trade. However, trade between India and Pakistan has always been linked to the political relations the two countries share, than being merely governed by economic factors. Following the independence and partition in 1947, Indo-Pakistan trade fell severely; and came to a standstill for almost nine years in the aftermath of the war in 1965. A protocol on carrying on of trading relations was signed in 1974 on a list of mutually agreed items. In 1996, India accorded Most Favored Nation (MFN) status to Pakistan thereby offering Pakistan the same trading regime as it offers to any other country in the world. Pakistan, on the other hand, continued to allow imports of a limited number of items from India, collectively known as the positive list; although the number of items on the list has increased gradually.[20] The grant of MFN was linked to the resolution on the Kashmir issue. Moreover, India stopped trade via the air and land routes between 2001 and 2004 following the attack on Indian parliament in December 2001. In 2013, for the first time since 2004, cross border trade was altogether stopped following the incidence of cross border firing; with trade resuming within a few days time. Restriction on trade had been on several other counts as well, with the major ones being:

a) a restrictive maritime protocol until 2005 which allowed only Indian and Pakistani flagged vessels to carry cargo between the two countries, and not permitting the same vessels to carry consignments to a third country from the ports of either, b) presence of only one rail route for cargo movement between the two countries; and c) Absence of road-based trade route until 2005. This restrictive trading environment resulted in large informal trade flows between India and Pakistan, with most of the trade taking place via third country ports such as Dubai. The process of trade normalization was set in motion in 2004 during the Commerce Secretary level talks on Commercial and Economic Co-operation between India and Pakistan. In this comprehensive dialogue, trade negotiations were to be discussed along with a dialogue on several other issues. This was the first step towards delinking trade negotiations from political issues. Since 2004, any major political event between India and Pakistan has neither met with any major impact on trading relations and bilateral trade has only been rising over the years.[21] In 2004, as members of the South Asian Association for Regional Cooperation (SAARC), India and Pakistan signed the South Asian Free Trade Agreement (SAFTA). The members of SAFTA include four least developed countries (LDCs) –Nepal, Bhutan, the Maldives, and Bangladesh; and three non-least developed countries (NLDCs) –India, Pakistan and Sri Lanka. SAFTA, as all other regional agreements under the WTO, required members to offer MFN treatment to each other. However, even after SAFTA was ratified in 2006, Pakistan did not accord MFN status to India and continued to trade on the positive list, allowing import of only 137 items from India via road, thereby making the route more restrictive.

Thus with the two largest SAARC countries not trading under MFN rules, SAFTA has failed at helping normalize trade relations between India and Pakistan.[22]

The bilateral trade dialogue that had started in 2004 continued for four more rounds of talks until 2007 and resulted in three major outcomes- expansion of the positive list, opening of the road route in 2005, and amendment of the restrictive maritime protocol. As part of the Confidence Building Measures, in October 2008 the two governments permitted trade and travel across the Line of Control along Jammu and Kashmir. Following the Mumbai attacks in November 2008, the composite dialogue was stalled. It resumed after a hiatus of three years. During these three years, however, no proactive measures were taken to block trade such as those initiated in response to the Parliament attack in 2001.

The fifth round of talks in April 2011 laid down the blueprint for normalizing trade between India and Pakistan. Perhaps what set the tone for the talks was the recognition of the necessity to promote bilateral trade to "build confidence, dispel misunderstandings and allay misapprehensions". While the agenda was very detailed (covering inter alia the MFN issue, addressing non-tariff barriers, improving border infrastructure, customs liaison, harmonization of customs procedures, trade in electricity and petroleum products, co-operation in information technology, visas, bilateral investments, and opening of bank branches) the two negotiating points revolved around Pakistan granting MFN status to India and the latter addressing nontariff barriers faced by Pakistan in accessing India's market. The Joint Statement issued in November 2011 laid down the sequencing and timelines for full phasing in of MFN status for India. In the first phase, Pakistan would graduate from the positive list to a small negative list specifying banned rather than permitted items. In the second stage, the negative list would be phased out; overall as well as for the road route on which trade takes place for only a fraction of the items on the positive list. These changes would usher in the full phasing in of MFN that forms an essential part of the trade normalization process.[23]

Adhering to the Joint Statement, in March 2012 Pakistan made a transition from the positive list approach to a small negative list of 1,209 items. However, it continued to restrict road-based trade by allowing only 137 items to be imported from India via road; while India took a number of steps to address Non Tariff Barriers (NTB's). Since then, trade negotiations on MFN changed stance one more time. During the 7th Round of talks held in September 2012, India and Pakistan agreed to further deepen the preferential arrangements under SAFTA with India offering concessions to Pakistan in exchange for Pakistan granting MFN status to India. In a major step, India pruned its sensitive list to 614 items. The current status as of July 2013 is that India would bring down its SAFTA Sensitive List to 100 tariff lines (from the existing 614 items); with Pakistan simultaneously granting MFN status to India, including the phasing out of negative lists and removal of restrictions on items traded by road.

Trade Potential and Possibilities

This section examine the current trade trends, assess trade potential for India and Pakistan, examine the composition of the negative and sensitive lists, and assess the extent of trade potential accounted for by these items. The protected sectors having the highest trade potential are identified and implications of opening up these sectors have been discussed. The sectors that are likely to face competition from imports once the negative and sensitive lists are further liberalized have also been identified. Trade possibilities and potential in the important service sectors have been examined as well.

Trends in Bilateral Trade

Bilateral trade between India and Pakistan increased by more than 9 times between the years 2000 and 2011. Total trade between the two countries was US$ 1.97 billion in 2011, of which India's exports to Pakistan were US$ 1.66 billion and imports US$ 313 million. Despite exporting only on the positive list, India has always had a trade surplus excluding mineral fuels with Pakistan; with the trade balance as a proportion of its total trade with Pakistan increasing from 55 to 68 percent between 2000 and 2011. However from 2009-12, the average annual rate of growth of imports from Pakistan has been 23 percent while that of exports has been just 9 percent, signaling some reversals in the trend. In 2011, India's top 3 exports to Pakistan at the classification of items included chemicals, textiles and vegetable products accounting for 68 percent of total exports to Pakistan. India's top 3 imports included mineral products, vegetable products and textiles accounting for 59 percent of total imports. At a disaggregated level, top commodities exported from India to Pakistan that year included, cotton, oil-cake, xylene, tomatoes, woven fabrics, chickpeas, polypropylene, rubber tyres, tea, fruits, and iron and steel containers. Cotton alone accounted for 16 percent of exports.

Trade Potential in Goods

Several estimates have been made to predict the trade potential between India and Pakistan. But despite lower inter-country distances, transport and other transaction costs of trading are very high. Moreover, existing bilateral trade is limited to the positive list. Trade possibilities exist in items that two countries can import from each other instead of importing from elsewhere in the world. The results of this exercise show the existence of an estimated untapped bilateral trade potential of US$ 19.8 billion in 2011, which is 10 times larger than the current US$ 1.97 billion trade. Of this export potential accounts for US$ 16 billion, and import potential US$ 3.8 billion. The potential in mineral fuels is another US$ 10.7 billion of which export potential accounts for US$ 9.4 billion and import potential US$1.3 billion. This analysis includes only those items in the trade potential exercise in which the partner country is globally competitive. The intuition behind this is that items with a revealed comparative advantage to export to the rest of the world are most likely to be traded between India and Pakistan if there are trade possibilities. The total trade potential excluding mineral fuels falls to US$10.9 billion with the export potential accounting for US$7.9 billion and import potential accounting for US$3 billion. The trade potential from mineral fuels remains almost the same at US$ 10.4 billion. For India and Pakistan this untapped potential lies between US$ 10.9 billion and US$ 19.8 billion, excluding mineral fuels. Mineral fuels account for an additional export potential of US$10.4 billion to US$10.7 billion. After excluding mineral fuels, it is find that the difference is mainly due to lower estimates in India's export potential to Pakistan. India's export potential to Pakistan for products with comparative advantage is much lower at US$ 7.9 billion which is almost half of the total export potential of US$ 16 billion obtained. This implies that India has a comparative advantage in about half of the commodities it can potentially export to Pakistan. On the other hand, the import potential does not differ much in the two approaches, indicating that Pakistan has a revealed comparative advantage in most of the products which can potentially be exported to India. The export and import potential for Pakistan's negative and sensitive list; and for India's sensitive list is also calculated. India's export potential for Pakistan's negative list items accounts for 43 percent of its total export potential; and items on Pakistan's sensitive list under SAFTA account for 33 percent of India's total export potential. Export potential of items that are either on Pakistan's negative list or on the SAFTA sensitive list account for 56 percent of India's total export potential. India's import potential from Pakistan for items on its sensitive list under SAFTA account for 22 percent of India's total import potential. Thus, a substantial proportion of India's export potential is in products that are either on Pakistan's negative list for India or on the sensitive list under SAFTA. Similarly, a significant proportion of India's import potential is in items on the sensitive list under SAFTA.

Thus, even if trade is normalized, the two countries are likely to have limited preferential access to each other's markets. However, what is interesting is that when the export potential calculated after including only those items for which India has a comparative advantage to export to the world, 60 percent of the difference in estimates of export potential obtained in the account of items on Pakistan's negative/sensitive lists. The inference that can be drawn is that India is not competitive in a significant proportion of items on Pakistan's negative/ sensitive lists, hence negating any rationale for these items to remain on Pakistan's negative/sensitive lists. Similarly, 68 percent of the difference in import potential that is observed after including only those items where Pakistan has a comparative advantage to export to the world, is accounted by items on India's sensitive list.

The three categories with the largest export potential from India to Pakistan are, textiles, chemicals, and machinery, mechanical appliances and electrical equipment accounting for 55 percent of total export potential. At a disaggregated level, largest potential items include petroleum oils, light petroleum oils, cellular phones, cotton, vehicle components, polypropylene, xylene, tea, textured yarn, synthetic fibre and medicaments. However, 13 of the top 25 products with the highest potential are currently on Pakistan's negative or sensitive lists or on both, making it difficult to realize the potential from these items. The three categories with the largest import potential include textiles, jewelry and precious metals, and base metals accounting for 52 percent of total import potential. At a disaggregated level the items with largest import potential include petroleum oils, jewelry, medical instruments and appliances, cotton, tubes and pipes of iron and steel, polyethylene , copper waste and scrap, structures and parts of structures, terephthalic acid and its salts, and sports equipment. Again 6 out of 25 products with the highest import potential are on India's sensitive under SAFTA.

India has a huge export potential in mineral fuels largely accounted for by petroleum oil and light petroleum oil. The potential for the former is US$ 7.7 billion and the latter is US$ 1.3 billion. India's import potential from

Pakistan in petroleum oils is US$ 1.3 billion. Although both countries have export potential in petroleum oils, analysis at a more disaggregated 8 digit level reveals that Pakistan's major petroleum oil export is base oil while India's comparative advantage is in high speed diesel, aviation turbine fuel, fuel oil and lubricating oil.

Negative and Sensitive Sectors

Pakistan's negative list of 1209 items is specified at the 8-digit level of classification followed by Pakistan Custom's Office. This classification differs from the Indian classification at the same level of disaggregation. Analysis of the 1209 items indicates that auto components account for 32 percent of the items, followed by steel and paper products accounting for 11 percent and 8 percent respectively. However, it needs to be mentioned that in the process of aggregation, some products which were not on the negative list at the 8 digit level, got included as well. Hence, there were 788 items on Pakistan's negative list. Five categories, namely auto, electrical machinery, textiles, steel and pharmaceuticals accounted for almost 90 percent of the export potential on the negative list, within which, auto alone accounted for around 30 percent of the export potential on the negative list. In addition, India's export potential in items that are included in Pakistan's negative list is largest in automobiles (included largely in the category vehicles, aircraft, vessels and transport) accounting for 12 percent of India's total export potential to Pakistan. To identify specific commodities on Pakistan's negative list that are 'vulnerable' to competition from imports, for every item traded between India and Pakistan. Thus in the automobile sector which accounted for the highest export potential on the negative list, out of a total of 167 items, only 35 were vulnerable as these were items in which India is globally competitive but Pakistan is not. Similarly in textiles, out of 74 items on the negative list, Pakistan is vulnerable only in 25, or 34 percent of the items. India's export potential in items that are included in Pakistan's sensitive list under SAFTA is largest in automobiles (included largely in the category vehicles, aircraft, vessels and transport) accounting for 37 percent of export potential of sensitive list items 12 percent of India's total export potential. However, out of 70 items on the sensitive list in this category, Pakistan is vulnerable in only 19 items. In terms of number of items, textiles sector was the largest accounting for 24 percent of total number of items on the Sensitive list. But these accounted for only 4 percent of India's export potential for items on Pakistan's sensitive list under SAFTA. Moreover, of the total 224 textile items on the sensitive list, Pakistan is likely to face competition in only 41, or 18 percent of the items. India's sensitive list under SAFTA has the largest number of items in the textiles sector which accounted for 30 percent of the total number of items on the sensitive list, while accounting for 62 percent of India's import potential for items on the sensitive list, and 14 percent of India's total import potential from Pakistan. Further, out of a total of 182 textile items on the sensitive list, India is vulnerable in only 45, or 25 percent of the items. It can hence be inferred that while Pakistan considers its automobile sector most susceptible to competition, India fears competition in the textile sector. However, the tendency for both countries has been to protect several tariff lines in which neither partner is competitive. In Pakistan the automobile sector is highly protected. The automotive industry was set up initially by Japanese, European and Korean manufacturers. These assemblers are supported by the auto component manufacturers or vendors. Some of the assemblers have joint ventures with the component manufacturers while others are independent. During 1985-2006 the industry adopted a 'Deletion Program' which mandated a compulsory localization of components over a period of time to provide protection to the local vendor industry.[24] In order to comply with WTO on Trade and Investment, the Deletion Program was abandoned but the sector continued to be protected by high tariffs. Pakistan currently imports completely-knocked down-kits (CKDs) and semi-knocked down kits (SKDs) from Japan, and parts from Thailand at higher prices than those from India. Opening of trade with India will make cheaper parts available to the industry. India's automobile vendor industry had a similar protected regime including an equivalent of Pakistan's Deletion Program for the automobile manufacturers. With continuous liberalization India has become a global R&D and small-car manufacturing hub. Indian auto component manufacturers on the other hand are moving up the value chain and delivering complex products though largely for the domestic market.[25] The Government's Automotive Mission Plan (AMP) 2006-2016 visualizes India moving up the value chain and entering into R&D, design and manufacture of automobiles and auto components. Pakistan can learn from India's experience of opening up the automobile and auto component industry. Moreover, one of the major factors for the significant performance improvement in Pakistan's motor cycle industry is attributed to the opening up of Pakistan's market to imported Chinese components.[26] Thus there is a case for Pakistan to further liberalize its auto sector. Currently, there is hardly any direct trade in auto components between

India and Pakistan and most of the trade is routed via Dubai, according to the Automotive Component Manufacturers Association of India.

On the other hand India's textile and clothing sector has been one of the most protected sectors in India. Until 2005, readymade garments were reserved for exclusive manufacture by small scale firms; large firms were not permitted to manufacture these items. To protect the domestic industry, textiles and readymade garments were also subjected to high import duties and specific duties which were applied in quantitative terms and not on ad-valorem basis. In fact some of the ad-valorem rates exceeded 300 percent. In 2005, the readymade garment items were removed from the reserved list thereby allowing large firms to enter into manufacturing. However, these items continued to be on the sensitive lists of India's free trade agreements even thought the rationale for protecting the industry was no longer there.[27] It was only in 2008 that India removed 164 textile items from the sensitive list for LDCs under SAFTA and offered duty free access. In 2011, all textile items were allowed duty free access from LDCs. Sri Lanka was offered duty free access to 215 textile items under the India-Sri Lanka Free Trade Agreement in 2008. Similarly, a complex system of subsidies and taxes oriented the mill sector (spinning and yarn) powerfully towards the small-scale power-loom based weaving sector, which in turn was oriented primarily towards domestic consumption.[28] In 2011-12, the mill sector accounted for only 5 percent of the total cloth produced by the mill and power loom sectors.[29]

However, there is a distinct difference in the fabric produced by the two sectors. While the mill sector produces high quality and high-value fabric, the fabric produced by the power looms is of low quality and commands a lower price. Pakistan on the other hand has a strong yarn and fabric manufacturing industry with India fearing is that imports from Pakistan would hurt its small and medium scale sector. Fabric imports from Pakistan are more likely to compete with the mill sector in India rather than the power loom sector thus providing no justification for India to protect the large firms from imports. Also, as noted above, India does not face much threat by opening up the Indian market to Pakistan's textile sector as only 25 percent of the textile items on India's sensitive list fall in the 'vulnerable' category. However it is agriculture that is the main point of contention in the ongoing trade talks. Even though farmers in Pakistan are raising concerns over unfair competition from Indian imports of agricultural products while they enjoy various subsidies, the negative list has very few agriculture items. India's export potential in tobacco items which are on negative list is less than 1 percent of the total import potential of items on the negative list. All the remaining agricultural items have been removed from the negative list. However, farmers fear that if the land route is opened to agricultural imports, then they would not be able to compete with Indian products.[30] Pakistan has always been concerned that due to high subsidies, the prices of agricultural commodities are lower in India and therefore opening up of trade would have a negative impact on the domestic producers. While India does offer subsidies, its non product specific subsidies are below 10 percent of the value of agricultural output, abiding by the WTO rules.[31] Further, it needs to be noted that prior to 1996 even when trade between the two countries was limited to a handful of items on the positive list, agriculture was part of this positive list, as it was not only an important means of overcoming short-term fluctuations but was also important for maintaining domestic price stability. At the time when Pakistan's positive list expanded to 1963 items, 156 agricultural commodities formed a part of this list. While Pakistan may have genuine concerns regarding any adverse impact on its agriculture sector due to a surge in agricultural imports from India, the solution should be to seek safeguards within the WTO system and under SAFTA, rather than imposing a total ban on agricultural commodities from India.

Trade Possibilities in Services

There are additional trade possibilities in services sector which is becoming increasingly important in the economies of India and Pakistan. In 2011-12, this sector accounted for 59 percent of India's GDP and 54 percent of Pakistan's GDP. Three sectors, where there is potential include information technology and Business Process Outsourcing (BPO), health services, and entertainment services. India's IT and BPO sector revenues were US$ 87.6 billion in 2011-12. Software exports in 2011-12 were US$69 billion compared to US$59 billion in 2010-11. Exports dominate the industry and constitute about 78.4 percent of total industry revenue. Indian IT service offerings have evolved from application development and maintenance to emerge as full service players providing testing and infrastructure services, consulting, and system integration.[32] The BPO sector which initially offered only low value services is now characterized by greater breadth and depth of services. Although the IT industry in Pakistan is in its infancy, it is growing at a fast pace. IT exports in 2011 were US$ 440 million, up from US$ 432 million in 2013 previous year. This is one of the potential areas which could be exploited as both countries are competing in information and information services. India and Pakistan can establish joint ventures. While Pakistan could provide professionals at lower wages, Indian companies could help in procurement of international contracts.[33] Pakistan is emerging as an exporter of specialized software services such as gaming and animation, financial services and healthcare, which Indian companies could import. The two countries could also gain if India sets training institutes in Pakistan, or if professionals from Pakistan come to India to get professional training. The BPO segment in Pakistan is also growing. Government incentives to the international outsourcing community include 100 percent equity ownership, 100 percent repatriation of capital and dividends, and income tax exemption for IT companies till 2016. India could collaborate with the BPO firms in Pakistan to offer more value added services in this segment.

Healthcare service is another area in which there are opportunities for both countries. India has emerged as an important destination for provision of medical services due to affordable cost of treatment and advancement in the field of medicines. Several Pakistani patients have been visiting India for medical treatment like liver transplant, open heart surgery and kidney transplant.[34] Other specialty treatment is also being offered to Pakistani patients. For instance, the Mumbai Obstetric and Gynecological Society is providing treatment for infertility to Pakistani couples. Despite a relatively tight visa regime, the number of patients coming from Pakistan to India is on the rise. According to a report, the Indian High Commission in Islamabad issued 1,992 medical visas to Pakistani citizens during 2008-2010. In addition, 2,917 visas were issued to medical attendants during the same period. There is a vast scope for cooperation in the health sector. In February 2012, a group of Indian and Pakistani doctors jointly performed a complicated liver transplant procedure in a Lahore hospital for the first time thereby opening new avenues for co-operation in the area of healthcare services.[35]

There are trade possibilities in the entertainment industry as well. India and Pakistan share a common language and culture, thus providing scope for trade and co-operation in the film industry. India is the second largest producer of movies in the world, while Pakistan produces very few movies. Pakistan had imposed a ban on screening of Indian films in 1965 following the Indo-Pak war. The purpose of the ban was largely to protect the domestic film industry. However, despite the ban the Pakistani film industry has not done well.[36] The ban was lifted in 2008, but since then there has been uncertainty in the policy as several ad-hoc steps have been taken to ban Indian movies on a case by case basis. Through the years, the ban has been practically ineffective as the demand for Indian movies in Pakistan is met through pirated DVDs and satellite cable broadcasts of Indian films. There is an interest in India and Pakistan for each other's music- both audio and visual. There is also an interest in Pakistan to watch Indian television serials and in India to watch Pakistani plays. However, Pakistani entertainment channels are not broadcasted on Indian channels whereas several Indian channels are broadcasted in Pakistan. The trade potential in the entertainment industry particularly in films, television and music can be tapped by encouraging joint productions. Removing the ban on screening movies would benefit both the countries. Exchanging broadcasting rights to telecast each other's programmes on television is yet another trade opportunity for India and Pakistan.

Transport and Transit

Most discussions and studies on the transport issue have focused on the impediments related to the land route. While the sea route has always been operational, it went unnoticed due to the restrictive maritime protocol. This protocol allowed only Indian and Pakistani flagships to carry cargo between India and Pakistan. This arrangement restricted competition from foreign vessels, and therefore resulted in high sea freight rates being charged by Indian and Pakistani vessels. The amendment of this protocol in 2005 brought sea trade between the two countries under global maritime arrangements, leading to greater competition, and therefore, to a considerable reduction in costs for sea-based trade between Mumbai and Karachi. It is not surprising that in 1995-96 when the road route was closed, trade by rail accounted for 63 percent while that by sea accounted for 33 percent of the total trade between India and Pakistan. By 2011-12 the share of different modes in total trade between the two countries changed substantially due to the opening of the road route and the liberalization of the sea trade. The share of trade by rail fell to 15 percent, while that by sea increased to 60 percent. Share of trade by road increased from zero percent in 1995-96 to 17 percent in 2011-12. Moreover, what is striking is that for both exports and imports, apart from a few commodities like dry dates and cements, most of the top commodities are traded via a single mode of transport, either road, rail, sea or air. The opening of the road route between India and Pakistan after 58 years was a historic move. India and Pakistan share a 2912 kilometer long border. The significance of this move can be better understood when compared with cross-border transport protocols that India has with Nepal. India and Nepal have the most liberal transport protocol which permits trucks from the two countries to move into each other's territories. This is because when trucks move from one country to the other, the local mafia extorts money from the foreign trucks.

Thus, transshipment continues to occur because these informal payments are higher than the cost of transshipment. Hence there is a need to strengthen institutions at the border for effective implementation of policies. On the other hand, the opening up of the road route between India and Pakistan has met with relatively little opposition. Indeed, the institutional framework supporting trade between the two countries is strong enough to counter lobbyists and interest groups that may have resisted such a change. This raises immense hopes for successful implementation of further trade-facilitating measures at the land border between India and Pakistan. Amritsar and Lahore are the two major cities on either side of the border separated by a distance of only 54 kilometers. Hence, the transport costs for goods moved via land route between northern India and northern Pakistan could be substantially lower than the sea route. Recognizing the importance of the land route, India opened an Integrated Check Post (ICP) at Attari in April 2012, with new facilities including a trade gate that would house all trade activities under one unit including warehousing and other facilities. Timings for trade were increased to 12 hours every day for all days of the week. While the ICP is operational, the two most important facilities that are underway include automated systems for electronic filing of customs documents through the Electronic Data Interchange (EDI) facility and installation of truck scanners. This is a marked change from the past, when there was only one gate for trade and for passengers, trade timings were limited to only 7 hours daily, and no warehousing facilities were offered. In a short span of just six months – between April and October 2012, the warehouse has reached full capacity. This in turn limits the entry of trucks from across the border. The question is whether these facilities will be able to bear additional cargo load which is likely to occur for two reasons- Pakistan's move to normalize trade on the road route by allowing all items to be imported from India via road, instead of the existing list of only 137 items; and a likely shift in trade from the sea to road route due to lower transaction costs in the latter. The ICP, when conceived by the Indian government clearly did not envisage such a paradigm change in trade between the two countries. The trade would increase further if the two governments agreed to move containerized cargo by road. Allowing these trucks to move in each other's territory is yet another measure that would reduce transaction costs further. The two governments are also considering opening up of new road routes. The option of opening the Munabhao- Khokhrapar road route was discussed in the seventh round of talks between the two governments.

The rail route was the dominant land-transport mode for India-Pakistan trade for several years. The rail route's relative importance over the sea and road route has declined as it continues to be limited in its reach. Goods transported by the goods train, often referred to as "interchange train", or by parcel wagons; are attached to the Samjhauta Express passenger train which runs on a biweekly basis carrying 6 to 10 parcel wagons. Since the capacity of Samjhauta Express is limited, most of the rail cargo is carried by the interchange train. Earlier studies have pointed out that the existence of only one rail route through the Attari/Wagah border, poor quality of rolling stock and restriction on the type of wagons are some of the problems that traders faced.[37] Also, traders in Kolkata, located in eastern India, find it difficult to trade through the Attari/Wagah land border because of lack of information on how to trade by the rail route. Therefore, they send consignments by sea to Colombo, which are then transshipped to Karachi.[38] Since 2007, there has been deterioration in interchange train services. Goods by the interchange train move only between Amritsar and Lahore through the Attari rail station, with just the Pakistani wagons plying on this route, unlike earlier when Indian wagons also plied on the rail route. Cargo for export either comes in Indian wagons up to Amritsar where it is unloaded and then loaded onto Pakistani wagons; or it is loaded on trucks to be sent through Wagah. Transshipment of cargo from Indian to Pakistani wagons or onto trucks adds considerable time and cost to transporting goods. Even though infrastructure has improved with the ICP, these facilities do not extend to rail cargo movement. The railway line is about three kilometers away from the ICP. The agenda for improving rail transport remains largely unaddressed. While the 7th round of talks agreed to increasing the number of interchanges to 3-4 in a day and allowing high capacity wagons to ply, the discussions so far have only covered the immediate needs of facilitating rail transport.

The ongoing bilateral dialogue between India and Pakistan has so far not addressed the issue of transit. India has not allowed Pakistan to access Nepal, Bangladesh, and Bhutan through its territory. Similarly, Pakistan has not given any transit rights to India to access Afghanistan for its exports. However, Pakistan offered transit rights to Afghanistan's exports through its territory to reach the Indian market in 1948. In July 2010, Afghanistan and Pakistan signed an amended transit trade agreement, the Afghanistan-Pakistan Transit-Trade Agreement (APTTA), which provides for an increased number of transport routes available to trucks from Afghanistan and Pakistan. However, the APTTA does not allow India's exports to Afghanistan through Pakistan via the land route. In order to increase their gains from the trade normalization process, India and Pakistan must put this transit issue on their dialogue agenda. This would also have huge implications for reviving the Afghan economy. Afghanistan can gain little through trade given its limited export capability but it can take advantage of its geographical location by converting into a logistic hub and offering a whole range of logistic services that could help transport goods between South and Central Asia. It follows that India should also allow transit facility to Pakistani goods for accessing the Nepal and Bangladesh markets. There is need to develop a long term vision and plan for road and rail cargo movement by the land route. Limiting the opening of the land route to just the land border is not enough. Freight costs are often determined by the freight trade balance between two countries. Since India has a trade surplus with Pakistan, India's cargo trucks/wagons moving back from Pakistan will not be fully loaded, with empty wagons adding considerably to transaction costs. However, if the trucks/wagons are allowed cross border movement and multimodal-transportation is permitted, cargo balancing could be achieved by linking the sea ports of Mumbai and Karachi through the land route, with the sea ports largely connecting the rest of the world. Similarly transit through Pakistan can link Indian sea ports with Afghanistan and to rest of Central Asia through Pakistan.

Non-Tariff Barriers

For many years Pakistani government has expressed that their businessmen face nontariff barriers in accessing the Indian market. On this issue, it was recognized by both countries during the talks that there were no Pakistan-specific barriers but a general lack of awareness amongst Pakistani businessmen on the regulatory regimes in India. In a study conducted in 2008 for the Task Force on Non Tariff Measures (NTMs) it was found that while these NTMs were not discriminatory, the procedures relating to product standards were cumbersome, some regulations lacked transparency, and there were problems related to recognition of standards. The two governments however felt that it was important to address the perceived barriers as well. In September 2011, the Indian government arranged interactive sessions between the Indian regulators and Pakistani businessmen in New Delhi to help increase awareness amongst the latter on India's regulatory policies. Such a session was subsequently held in Pakistan in January 2012.[39] This government-to-business interaction is an innovative and effective method of addressing information gaps on the regulatory environment of India and Pakistan.

Recently, the Trade Development Authority of Pakistan supported experts to undertake a study that identified potential products for exports to India, including tariff and nontariff barriers that Pakistani businessmen faced. The findings of the study were subsequently disseminated across ten cities in Pakistan to inform the businesses on India's regulatory regimes. Some of the reported barriers included over valuation of goods, tedious packaging and labeling requirements, access to limited number of ports for some products, lack of testing facilities at ports, inadequate infrastructure, mishandling of goods, and theft of cargo at ports. Businesses were also educated on the use of WTO compliant trade defense instruments and how they could be used to restrict imports which could hurt the domestic industry. Such a government supported awareness initiative, if done on a sustained basis every few years, could have a long term impact on dispelling notions and misconceptions of perceived barriers amongst businessmen willing to access the Indian market. It shall also help in raising awareness on genuine non-tariff barriers, and equipping businesses to deal with expanded imports if they hurt their domestic industry. In another initiative to address non-tariff barriers, Governments of India and Pakistan signed three agreements in September 2012; including a customs cooperation agreement to help avoid arbitrary stoppage of goods at each other's ports, a bilateral cooperation agreement on mutual recognition between 'Pakistan Standard and Quality Control Authority (PSQCA)' and 'Bureau of Indian Standards (BIS)'; and an agreement on redressal of trade grievances between Pakistan and India. Non-tariff barriers of a different nature were identified in some studies.[40] It was found that Pakistani consignments were subjected to excessive checks- usually due to security concerns causing harassment to genuine traders. Marketing and labeling issues relating to the perceived 'image' of Pakistani goods was also pointed out in recent studies. For instance, the label on Pakistani bed linen was changed to European and Indian labels for sale in the Indian market. Holding exhibitions, such as the Pakistan Mega Lifestyle Exhibition held in Delhi in April 2012 and the Made in Pakistan Expo held in August 2012 in Mumbai, could aid acceptance of Pakistani goods in India. In September 2012, the Pakistan Fashion Design Council opened an outlet in an up-market shopping complex in New Delhi. Such steps will certainly raise awareness among Indian consumers about Pakistani products. Indian products too face a labeling issue, with their Pakistani counterparts advising on dropping the 'Made in India' label to accentuate sales in Pakistan. However, newer products such as sweets and snacks, manufactured by a large Indian firm, have made a successful entry in the Pakistani market under the Indian label. Though measures to mitigate NTB's have been undertaken, addressing them is not a one-time effort. India and Pakistan need to identify, deal with, and address new NTB's on a continuous basis, as and when they are raised.

Informal Trade

The restrictive trade environment, has led to large informal trade flows between India and Pakistan, estimated to range from US$ 250 million to US$ 3 billion. The most detailed study on Indo-Pakistan informal trade estimated its value at around US$ 545 million in 2005.[41] Pakistan's imports from India are estimated to be around US$ 535 million and exports to India US$ 10.4 million. The main import items from India, via informal channels, are cloth, tires, pharmaceuticals, textile, machinery, cosmetics, livestock and medicines; accounting for roughly 80 percent of total informal import value. Pakistan's informal exports mainly consist of textiles; accounting for approximately 90 percent of the total informal trade. It is interesting to note the modalities of India-Pakistan informal trade, with most of the trade flowing via third country. Khan estimates trade via Mumbai-Dubai- Karachi route to be around 88 percent of total informal trade, and the remaining as cross border informal trade through the Amritsar-Lahore and Sind-Rajasthan border routes.[42]

However, almost 51 percent of informal trade taking place via Dubai does not reach Karachi directly as goods are transshipped from India to Dubai from where they are shipped to Bandar Abbas in Iran and then moved further via land across Afghanistan, to finally reach Pakistan. Only about 18 percent of informal trade takes place through the sea route from India to Karachi via Dubai. While these estimates are dated, they provide useful insights into the functioning of informal trade markets. It is reasonable to assume that individuals trading through the informal channels have devised parallel institutional mechanisms for contract enforcement and dispute settlement. Also, the smooth functioning of such markets shows that traders have developed efficient mechanisms for obtaining information on quantities and commodities to be traded and mitigating risks that might arise in the unofficial transacting environment.[43]

The move towards trade normalization and a parallel reduction in tariffs and non-tariff barriers would certainly lower informal trade flows between India and Pakistan. Trade through Dubai is likely to decrease sooner if there are active channels of information that would bring buyers and suppliers on either side together in order to conduct trade directly with each other rather than through third parties. Elimination of the negative list would also allow export of many items that had to be routed via Dubai and other informal channels of trade. Until all such measures are fully implemented, informal and formal trade between India and Pakistan are likely to co-exist.

Visas

A lot needs to be done in simplifying the visa regime between India and Pakistan. Grant of city-specific visa, the requirement of police reporting on arrival and before departure, the restriction on going beyond the port of entry, and delays in getting a visa have limited market access for aspiring traders. Consulates in both countries have exercised tremendous discretionary power in granting visas and waiving visa requirements along with allowing some traders to be exempted from scrutiny by the Ministry of Home Affairs in India and Ministry of Interior Affairs in Pakistan. They have also allowed extended period of stay, exempted Interviews with traders in Dubai in 2012 traders from police reporting, and removed restrictions on the number of cities that can be visited. Selected traders who are beneficiaries of such largesse can make repeated visits and enhance their Pakistan specific trade information; which remains inaccessible for other aspiring traders due to restricted market access, lack of transparency, market imperfections, and information asymmetries. However, Indian officials argue that, for the sake of security, rigorous screening of visas is essential. While it is true that no compromise can be made on national security issues, it needs to be recognized that genuine traders often become victims of a strict visa regime. The new visa agreement was signed between India and Pakistan in September 2012. The agreement introduces measures to ease travel of tourists, pilgrims, elderly and children to facilitate people-to-people contact between the two countries. The business visa has also been made more liberal, allowing one year multiple entry visas for upto 10 places with exemption from police reporting for those reporting a turnover of at least Rs. 30 million or equivalent in Pakistani Currency. The new visa regime is a step forward towards easing the channel for information exchange on trade-related matters between India and Pakistan. As a next step the countries could consider the use of electronic systems that would assist in having adequate and effective security systems in place while at the same time allowing genuine traders to trade across borders.[44]

Institutions Engaged in Trade Normalization

Trade normalization efforts have been driven at multiple levels on sides of India and Pakistan. All bilateral talks are spearheaded by the Ministry of External Affairs. Other important government departments involved are the Ministry of Commerce and the Ministry of Home Affairs. The former is leading the trade negotiating agenda while the latter has the primary responsibility of maintaining security. In India, two key functions performed by the Home Ministry in the context of trade include issuance of visas and border management. As part of its border management functions, Land Ports Authority of India (LPAI) was set up in April 2012 to provide cohesive management of cross-border movement of people and goods. On the side of Pakistan, the road port is managed by the National Logistics Cell, which falls under the purview of the Ministry of Defence. With respect to their bilateral visa regime, the Ministry of Home Affairs in India and Pakistan have taken progressive steps. The bureaucracy in India, arranged in vertical and hierarchical levels, seems to have accepted the pace of change set in motion by the trade normalization process. Even though, the issue of cross border terrorism often appears in bilateral talks, so far there has been no attempt to link it to the trade agenda. The Indian and Pakistani military forces are also not seen as adversaries in the trade normalization process. The involvement of NGO's too is quite limited. The business communities in both countries have been actively engaged in pursuing the trade liberalization agenda through the Chambers of Commerce for several years. In India, the Federation of Indian Chambers of Commerce and Industry (FICCI), the Confederation of Indian Industry (CII), the Associate Chambers of Commerce (ASSOCHAM), and the Punjab, Haryana and Delhi Chambers of Commerce and Industry (PHDCCI) have taken the initiative to facilitate cross border interactions between business delegations and communities to assess trade possibilities. Since the Summary Of Proceedings, Regional Chambers of Commerce Roundtable, Lahore January 10, 2013 initiation of the trade normalization process, such cross-border interactions have increased manifolds.

Academic discourse in India has largely focused on the political issues between India and Pakistan to have implications on trade normalization between the two countries. Until recently, the print and visual media too were engaged largely in 'negative' reporting as there was a tendency to report conflict rather than any peace initiatives undertaken by the two sides. Even the proposed grant of MFN status did not make headlines in any of the major news dailies. There is however, an evident shift towards positive reporting in the media on peace initiatives and trade co-operation which can have a huge impact on the perceptions of civil society towards relations shared by India and Pakistan.[45]

What is Immediately Required?

One of the most strategic issues needs immediate attention is MFN. On the issue of the Most Favored Nation (MFN) status and other trade requirements, India in principle granted MFN treatment to Pakistan in 1995-96 but has no list of permitted or forbidden products. Pakistan has not extended normal GATT/WTO rights or the MFN in principle to India, but maintains a `permissible list' of 600 items that may be legally imported from India. A glance at the permissible items indicates that most of items are chemicals, minerals and metal products. The finished products are not part of this list which should have been the part of list and that are the backbone of trade. Added to this, the items that are part of permissible list but invite a high tariff are cardamom, tea and electrode of graphite. There are non-tariff barriers on the items like beedi wrapper leaves, cardamom, tea, ginger (fresh) and synthetic organic coloring agents.

Emerging Issues:

The most vital and strategic issues to be resolved between India and Pakistan are lack of road trade routes, irregular railway traffic and an expensive shipping route. These issues are required immediate attention of both the countries. If these issues are not solved there are chances that global competitiveness would in danger as the cost of trade would go enormously. Further under South Asia Preferential Trading arrangement (SAPTA), India has extended to Pakistan tariff concessions on 393 items up to third round of SAPTA, but Pakistan has provided to India tariff concessions only on 248 items. But 73 of these 248 items cannot be imported from India as they are on the banned list... Further, not much headway has been made in any of the initiatives like SAPTA, SAFTA, Investment Promotion and Protection Treaty, Arbitration, and Regional Motor Vehicular Treaty, etc are essential for speedy growth in Indo-Pakistan Economic Relations. There should not be "myth" but "reality" in this regard. Corporate leaders are more capable of rewriting history than the political leadership of both India and Pakistan. People or a media-led civil society movement is also critical as people are the most important stakeholders and their will needs to be galvanized. India and Pakistan are living in unpredictable times with the international system in a constant state of flux on several horizons that is further endangering the international security system. It is imperative to create interdependence and partnership based on solid bedrock of commerce so that business ties act as a check to Government's initiating hostile action. Burden of peace is heavier on South Asia as it houses half the world's poor. Peace is no longer a luxury but a prerequisite that every member of the country or society needs to strive for. While responsibility rests heavier on the privileged, changing the public mindset requires initiatives from the full spectrum of society. Industry has an important role and contribution in brining an improvement in relationships and bilateral linkages. There is an immediate need to permit transit trade to Afghanistan and Central Asia, replace the positive list with a negative list of goods beyond which it would permit imports from India and improve its infrastructure for trade and transport.

South Asia is the least integrated region compared to East Asia, Latin America, Europe and Central Asia, Middle East and North Africa or sub-Saharan Africa. Other successful regional cooperation and integration initiatives have demonstrated that regional cooperation is a win-win and positive-sum situation that is beneficial to the entire region. There is no reason why SAARC nations in general and India and Pakistan in particular can not replicate such a model which has become sine-quo-non. It is true in all senses that geographical proximity offers tremendous scope to reap the benefits of cheaper transportation costs and trade complementarily in goods in which either country has a comparative advantage. Despite the shadow of two world wars and the cold war, unparalleled development has taken place in the last years. The sky is the limit for expansion of bilateral economic activity. Let us together step out of the old and into new.

Strategy for Future:

There is an urgent need for evolving an action plan on the following guide posts.

a) Keep up the continuous efforts for the grant of the MFN status by Pakistan to India as early as possible. Heavens have not fallen as a result of Pakistan not granting the status so far. Heavens would not shine on India, if it does. It is a matter of give and take. But it is a psychological weapon which India has for projecting Pakistan to the international community as an unreasonable power. Intensify the interactions with those sections of the Pakistani business community which are in favor of an early normalization of the business relations in order to step up pressure on Islamabad from its own business class. Keep the talks going on the pipeline issue without any illusions regarding its early and smooth implementation? b) Identify those areas of cooperation which could be projected to Pakistan as stand-alone areas. In one of his statements in India, Prime Minister of Pakistan has been quoted as referring to cooperation in the field of agriculture between Indian and Pakistani Punjab's, as another possible stand-alone area which Pakistan would be prepared to take up without linking it to the Kashmir issue? Pakistan's agriculture has not been doing as well as that of India as India is self-sufficient, forcing Pakistan to import wheat periodically. This is an area which needs to be explored intensively and extensively. A breakthrough in this direction is the need of the day. c) Planner and Policy makers both in India and Pakistan, as well as influential sectors of political and economic elite are also aware of the considerable potential of Indo-Pakistan economic and technological cooperation in areas of "mutually beneficial commonalties" that have come up in the wake of business liberalization (NEP). d) To exploit and capitalize the potential and opportunities arising out of changed political and economic environment. Governments in both nations must demonstrate their resolve to incrementally revise of fiscal policies that have prevented the flow of human capital and knowledge exchange wherein peoples and ideas across their national borders be exchanged, as they are major constraints in the way of the needed economic and technological collaboration. e) Intensify the interactions with those sections of the Pakistani business community which are in favour of an early normalization of bilateral economic relations. f) Identify areas of cooperation. Pakistan's agriculture has not been doing as well as that of India. Pakistan has to import wheat periodically while India is self-sufficient in food grains. This is an area which needs to be explored intensively and extensively, for a possible co-operation as hinted by the Pakistan's Prime Minister. g) Governments in both the countries must demonstrate their resolve to revise official policies that have prevented the flow of human capital and knowledge exchange.

Footnote

1. Ibid, p.2.
2. The Special Economic Zones Act 2012.

3. I. Nabi, "Pakistan's Trade with India: Thinking Strategically", Pakistan-India Trade: What needs to be done? What does it matter?, The Wilson Centre, Washington D.C, 2013.
4. The News International, September 27, 2013, at http://www.thenews.com., Accessed April 1, 2014.
5. Economic survey 2012–13, Ministry of Finance, Government of India, 2013, and, Economic survey 2012–13, Ministry of Finance, Government of Pakistan, 2013.
6. S.T. Hussain, "Trade in agriculture with India: View from Pakistan", India-Pakistan Trade Newsletter, ICRIER, 2013.
7. Wall Street Journal (2011, September 27). Big Pakistan mine draws fresh government objections.
8. Asia Times (2010, January 12). Balochistan halts $3.5bn copper project. Available at http://www.atimes.com/atimes/South_Asia/LA12Df03.html.
9. BioCon (2007, January 18). .Biocon grants exclusive marketing license for BiomapEGFR for Pakistan, Press Release 20 Available at http://www.biocon.com/biocon_inv_press_releases_18jan.asp
10. Kaul, S. (2013). India-Pakistan energy mutual interdependence: win-win strategy. Centre of Policy Initiatives & Energy Studies.
11. Lama, M. (2013) India-Pakistan energy cooperation: Rethinking opportunities and newer approaches. India Pakistan Trade Newsletter, 5–7. Available at http://www.indiapakistantrade.org/pdf/India-Pakistan-newsletter-13June.pdf. Accessed April 1, 2014.
12. Business Recorder (2014, January 22). Pakistan, India inch forward towards 500 megawatts power deal.
13. World Bank Logistics Performance Index, 2012, at www.woldbank.org.
14. Husain, I. (2011). Prospects and challenges for increasing India-Pakistan trade. Washington D.C.: Atlantic Council. Available at http://ishrathusain.iba.edu.pk/speeches/New/Atlantic_Council_Issue_brief_IndiaPakistanTrade.pdf. Accessed April 1, 2014.
15. Taneja, N., Mehra, M., Mukherjee, P., Bimal, S. & Dayal, I. (2013). Normalizing India-Pakistan trade. ICRIER Working Paper 267. New Delhi: ICRIER.
16. Ahmad, M. (2012, May 7). Vast scope for health sector cooperation. The News International.
17. Husain, I. (2012). Prospects, Challenges and Risks for Increasing India-Pakistan Trade. IBA Working Paper No. 1. Available at http://research.iba.edu.pk/workingpaper/DrIshratworkingpaperseries.pdf

18. Brada, J.C., Kutan, A.M., & Yigit, T.M. (2005). The effects of transition and political instability on foreign direct investment in ECE emerging markets. United Nations Economic Commission for Europe (UNECE), Spring Seminar. World Bank (2011). More and better jobs in South Asia. Washington, D.C.: The World Bank.
19. Vaqar Ahmed, India-Pakistan Trade Newsletter, October 2012, ICRIER, p.5.
20. Nisha Taneja and Others, "Normalizing India Pakistan Trade", Working Paper no. 267, September 2013, ICRIER.
21. Ibid.
22. Ibid.
23. Ibid.
24. USAID and Government of Pakistan (2007), "Policy Analysis on Competitive Advantage of Automotive Vendor Industry in Pakistan," May, Islamabad.
25. http://www.ibef.org.
26. Gary Pursell et. al. (2011), "Pakistan's Trade Policies: Future Directions", Working Paper 11/0361, IGC, London
27. Taneja N., Ray S., Kaushal N., Chowdhury D.R. (2011), "Enhancing Intra-SAARC Trade: Pruning India's Sensitive List under SAFTA", Working Paper No. 255, ICRIER, New Delhi.
28. Tewari, M (2005), "Post-MFA adjustments in India's Textile and Apparel Industry: Emerging Issues and Trends", Working Paper No. 167, ICRIER.
29. Government of India (2011-12), "Economic Survey", Ministry of Finance
30. Bhutta, Zafar (2012) "Duty free imports: Farmers fear they will lose in the import deal with India", The Express Tribune, November 16
31. Hoda, A. and Gulati, A. (2013), "India's Agricultural Trade Policy and Sustainable Development Goals"
32. Government of India (2011-12), "Economic Survey", Ministry of Finance
33. Husain, I. (2011), "Prospects and Challenges for Increasing India-Pakistan Trade", Atlantic Council
34. Ahmad, M. (2012), "Vast scope for health sector cooperation", The News International, May 7.
35. Times of India (2011), "India, Pakistan doctors perform joint liver transplant in Lahore", February 11.
36. The Express Tribune (2012), "Should Indian films be banned in Pakistan", July 25. Retrieved from http://tribune.com.pk/story/412954/should-indian-films-bebanned-in-pakistan/

37. Taneja, N. (2006), "India Pakistan Trade", Working Paper No. 182, Indian Council for research on International Economic Relations, New Delhi
38. Taneja, N. (2007), "Trade Possibilities and Non-tariff Barriers to Indo-Pak Trade", Working Paper No. 200, Indian Council for research on International Economic Relations, New Delhi
39. Taneja N., Ray S., Kaushal N., Chowdhury D.R. (2011), "Enhancing Intra-SAARC Trade: Pruning India's Sensitive List under SAFTA", Working Paper No. 255, ICRIER, New Delhi.
40. Taneja, N. (2007), "Trade Possibilities and Non-tariff Barriers to Indo-Pak Trade", Working Paper No. 200, Indian Council for research on International Economic Relations, New Delhi
41. Khan, Rafi S., Yusuf M., Bohkari S., and Aziz S. (2007),"Quantifying Informal Trade between Pakistan and India", In Naqvi Zareen Fatima and Philip Schuler, eds. 'The Challenges and Potential of Pakistan India Trade'
42. Ibid.
43. Taneja, N. (2004), "Informal Trade in the SAARC Region: Implications for FTAs",
44. Economic and Political Weekly, December 18.
45. -----------
46. -----------

5

Cultural Relations

In a broad sense, a culture cannot be developed. It emerges over time. It may change and evolve. It seems that it is not possible to talk of a society without talking about its culture, the development of society is not only about economics and finance, but also about how developed its culture is.[1] Pakistan and India share the same and common cultural history, food, language, dress and are tied with the upheaval of the invaders and colonial powers of the past as well. There cannot be two more similar people in other areas of the world.[2] As it was Muslims from whom the Britain took charge. Both countries blame each other for all the massacre and destruction caused at the time of partition and do not realize that the same incidents were found on both sides. The citizens of both countries remain strongly interrelated and interconnected with each other through the similar culture, weathers, festivities and traditions which are bonding them together despite the diplomatic differences promoted by the states.[3] The Social and cultural relationship with Pakistan is also an area which matters to concerns the emotions and belief of a common man. Similar people with common history can be the biggest enemies because the hurt of a perceived betrayal is the most. Emotion rules over the reason. Minorities of the both nations like Hindus in Pakistan and Muslims in India are still not mingled up and attached with the society in which they live. Contradictions and confusion on territory were compounded with similar flaws on the crucial issue of the minorities. Both states would be majoritarian states, a muslim state and a hindu state. Jinnah's words that "freedom for Hindu India as well as Muslim India ... you will protect and safeguard our minorities in your zones and we will protect and safeguard your minorities in our zones."[4] After the partition Jinnah was urged them to be loyal to their own state.

However being a large number like 170 million Muslims in India enjoy an equal right to cast their vote and have to come counted. They influence elections in Lok Shabh and the backward among them have been able to get reservation like Other Backward Classes (OBCs). But the problem of Hindus in Pakistan, said to be some 7 million, is that they are not large enough to have any say in political matters, nor are they content with they have been reduced to after partition[5]. But the religion of two Hindu girls and a Boy changed in August 2012 and forcefully married them with Muslims by some extremists group and there was a live telecast of this incident also but there was no steps taken by the Pakistan governments. This kind of situation creates gap and distance in efforts of establishing stable peace in the region.

Although India is socially, politically and economically better than Pakistan and had made remarkable progress in all spheres as compared to Pakistan, but there remains a stigma and chances of reconciliation in all regards with its neighbouring country; Pakistan. Following is the analysis of India Pakistan cultural relationship in term of literature, cricket, pilgrimage and education along with some suggestions for improvement of ties for the future.

Literature, History and Text Books

In the India –Pakistan context hate has all displaced love everywhere but in literature the very essence of its love, peace and humanism. If these qualities are absent it is just a piece of writing not literature. The creative writer has filled the gaps often left by historian, political analysts and sociologists. The most authentic and heart-rending accounts of the partition are to be found in the writings of Urdu writer Saadat Hasan Manto and those of his tribe, no matter what language they were writing in. Manto with his stories like 'Mutari', 'Mozelle', 'Thanda Gosht', 'Khol Do', 'Toba Tek Singh', is almost synonymous with partition and the horrors of communal violence it wrought. At the time of partition in 1947, Pakistan shared the literary culture of Indian subcontinent, which had a long history and a distinguished reputation.[6]

Writers and poets make efforts to set a platform to bringing people together from the both side of the border. Poets and fiction writers expressed remorse at the partition and purged the spirit by taking the blame long ago. Literature follows life, but now at happy moment we see life following literature. One just has to go to the literature of the two countries to see many memorial to Partition and also an effort to come together again. Ustad Daman was a true product of the oral tradition, a poet of baaghs (gardens). Put behind bars by all rulers for reciting his poetry in public places, his only book was published posthumously by his friends and pupils. His verses made an effort to bridge the gaps that has been caused by the politics of the time[7]:

Barbad inha azadian ton hoye tusi vi ho hoye assee vi haan

Lutan wale ne raj ke lutea hai soye tusi vi so soye assee vi saan

Laali akhiyan di payi dasadi hai roye tusi vi ho roye assee vi haan

(We were ruined in the name of freedom and so were you/ we were looted unawares for we were asleep and so were you/ the reddish eyes reveal that we have wept and so have you.)

Coming down on the politics of conflict and war as also of divide and rule, he says[8]:

Wahge naal Attari dee naeen takar, na geeta naal quran de aaye

Naaee kufr islam da koi jhagra sari gal nafe nuksan dee aay.

(The battle is not between Wagah and Attari/ Nor is it between the Gita and Quran/ There is no quarrel between the infidels and Islam/ It all boils down to politics of profit and loss.)

In the same tradition of reconciliation and remorse is the poem of Pakistani poet Munir Niazi called 'Honi de Heele'('Dirge to Destiny'):

Kis da dos si, Kis da nahi, eh galan hun karan dian nahi

Wele lang gaye tauba waale, raatan hauke bhardian nahi

Jo hoya eh hona hi si, te honi rokean rukdi nahi

Ik waari jadon shuru ho jaye, te gal phir aiven mukadi nahin

Kujh unjh vi raahvan aukhian san, kujh gal vich gham da tauk vi si

Kujh sher de log vi zalim san kujh sanu maran da shauk vi si

(who was at fault and who was not is not something to be discussed now/ The troubled times are long past and nights no longer pass sighing/ what happen had to happen for destiny takes its toll/ once something starts happening it cannot just be stopped/ the path was somewhat difficult and sorrow sat on our heart/ the people of the city were cruel, no doubt, but we too nurtured a death wish.)

A parallel in Pakistan to poetry written thus in the board left of the road progressive tradition is of Urdu poet Nasir Kazmi[9]:

Yeh zamin bat gayi, asman bat gaya, tarze tehreer, tarze bayan bat gaya

Shakhe gul bat gayi, ashian bat gaya, aur natije me Hindustan bat gya

(The earth was divided and so was the sky, our way of speaking and talking was divided/ The branches of the tree were divided and so also the nest/ The result was that Hindustan was divided.)

It is amusing indeed when politician come forward while presiding over literary meets and ask writers to write for peace. Perhaps they confuse writing with journalism that thrives more on conflict. A Punjabi satirist made an angry comment at the ruling elite saying that you start the fire and we are supposed to extinguish it, we are poets not fire brigades! Hindi poet Kumar Vikal derided the politicians who hurl their countries into war to just appear tall. The 1971 Indo-Pak war and the creation of Bangladesh evoked the most painful dirge from an East Punjabi poet Sohan Singh Misha:

Ajab hai ai dushmani di dastan, ghair nu dasiye te ho jaye hairan

Terian faujan ne jad merian faujan agge si hatihair suttee

Gile wargi gal si kujh rosh vi si , tu te royea hoyenga rohana hi si

Mere kyon atharoo si vage....

The Hindu-Muslim theme continued to recur in the stories and poems of Indian and Pakistani writers. Names of the writer and examples of their work from both countries would be endless.

But in school textbooks, It is also due to the wrong and biased description of the past in the history books written by writers of both countries only to insult each other and bring glory to its heroes. Most of the text books taught in the educational institutions of both countries also present false and subjective image so the nation grew up thinking each others as rivals and enemies. In order to invoke nationalism and making people proud of their past, the syllabus taught in the schools was rewritten to present facts and truths as a glory of one nation.[10] For example in the textbooks of India has highly slanted and prejudied view of minorities, particularly Muslims, Pakistani textbooks are no different. They are also designed as to promote hatered against Hindus and India. The powers that be in the both the countries have vested interest in keeping the hatred between the communities alive so as to beniefit politicaly from it. The seeds of hatred are sown in the young minds through these textbooks.[11] This kind of knowledge was designed to create hatred and violence against religious and national fragments gave birth to many episodes of tensions among the people of the country in India and Pakistan like the incidents of demolishing of Babri Masjid and Gujrat massacre in 2002 in India and this leads to destruction of many temples in Pakistan subsequently.[12]

Role of Cinema:

The cinema is no exception which can promote peace and solidarity among the masses. The popularity of Hindi cinema in India and large parts of Pakistan is widely recognized, and so is the idea that this popularity makes it a cultural force of unspecified strength in improving civil relations between the two nations. It is believe that an individual's relationship as a viewer with movies is rather more complicated and more interesting than we like to admit. When viewers sit down two watch movies like, *Veer Zara, Heena, Main Hoon na, Lakshaya, Pinjar, Gadar, Earth/1947, Hum Aapke Hain Kaun, Slumdog Millionaire, Jai Ho, Ek Tha Tiger* and so on, get some ideas of where these states are coming from. Cinema, more specifically, the Kind of film stories and characters that capture imagination and hearts of the masses, are also points where tradition and aspiration meet.[13] The Indian and Pakistani Diaspora has 'carried' undivided India along with to numerous countries around the globe and used it as an identity kit in foreign lands, especially the film and music germs. They (Indian, Pakistani, Bangladeshis) infect abroad in such a way as to bring them together, that creating a broader virtual identity--- the South Asian. In the periods of more than eight decades (1931-2014) of filmmaking, music composition and film watching have appealed to the large audiences in countries like India, Pakistan Bangladesh and etc. in that context the continued popularity of Bollywood's Hindi-Urdu hybridism over the last eighty three years acquires a much deeper significance. It is a significance that demands to be studied and understood. It is clear that at the time of watching movie in cinema a subterranean meeting of hearts and minds take place, and this meeting respects no borders. These clandestine Indo-Pak meetings with bollywood's stories and songs happen almost every week and what has this affair done to the great Indo-Pak conflict? It has kept alive an unacknowledged emotional bond at a person to person level, between political enemies.[14] Indian cinema and Music had made a tremendous progress in the last century as compared to Pakistani cinema. The artists and singers of Pakistan in order to get work and recognition started working in the Indian films and dramas and the Indian films also found a way in the cinemas of Pakistan. The Hindi-Urdu hybridism mentioned earlier is not just a language thing, it is a cultural thing, and experience thing. It is not a matter simply of promoting Hindu-Muslim brotherhood on screen. Often enough, the film appeal to audiences and their emotional bond on both sides. Although the films of India has ever been popular in Pakistan and the heroes of Indian film industry were praised and loved by Pakistanis long before the state give permission for the broadcasting of Indian channels officially. The songs of Indian films can be heard in almost every household of Pakistanis and even the shopping malls, in common day transportation vehicles and also in rural areas of Pakistan.[15] India wins Oscar in 2009 for its film Slumdog Millionaire and its musician A R Rehman also got awards for the making of its music and song Jai Ho at the 81st Academy Awards. Another Oscar came to the region in 2010, this time to Pakistan by Sharmeen Obaid-Chinoy who won Academy victim women in Pakistan.[16]

Changing hearts through Art and Theatre:

A artist believe that culture the arts and creative media in general present many opportunities for the promotion of the understanding of human rights and for forging unity amongst the peoples of India and Pakistan. Dance, music, visual and performing arts transcend language barriers and serve as incredible, almost magical means of communication and bonding. It must be noted that those people who came to watch cultural programmes may not necessarily be already converted to the ideas and objectives of the peace movement and, therefore, the whole concept of raising awareness and bringing people together through cultural inputs becomes that much more meaningful and effective. The arts and creative media can be used to communicate information and provide very real means of raising awareness about rights in a situation of conflict, they give people and communities a voice, and they offer a forum for the discussion of sensitive issues.[17]

Tehrik-e- Niswan was formed in 1980. Its main aim was to try and integrate art and politics with especial emphasis on women's right. In a society where there is conflict, art, if it is truthful, must also reflect the conflict and the decay. Whenever Tehrik sets out to produce a work of art, be it dance or drama, this world outlook, this ideology and highly conscious rational process is kept in mind. Some of these ideas are:

- To create awareness and change moral attitudes, especially about relations between India and Pakistan, and between Hindu and Muslim,
- to fight obscurantism and all kinds of fundamentalism, especially religious fundamentalism,
- to empower the oppressed people of India and Pakistan so that they

take control of their lives and try to bring about a social change, and

- to create an atmosphere of peace and harmony between the people of the two countries.

It feel that art and culture can do this because there is something in art that express an unchanging truth and has a liberating quality.[18]

The very first theatre production of tehirk-e- Niswan in 1980 was an adaptation of Safdar Hasmi's Play Aurat(Women). This play short vignettes on the lives of women in different classes. This was the first sharing experience between Indian and Pakistani artists. Another feminist play was adapted from the short stories of Amrita Pritam in 1981. The collection of stories was entitled Dard Kay Faslay (Miles of Pain), it shows that there was a hardly any different in the life and problem of female characters of both side. In 1988, prime minister Rajive Gandhi's visit to islamabad to meet his counterpart Benazir Bhutto. India and Pakistan sined a cultural accord that Pakistani and Indian artists would be given scholarships through an exchange programme between the two countries.[19] Since then tehrik and Ajoka (formed in 1984, it was christened Thertre for Social Change) performed continuosly on the stories of Indian and Pakistani writers like Anji by Vijay Tendulkerin 1985, Need kyu Raat Bhar Nahi ati (Why can't I sleep at night), Samjhaoon tou samjha na sakhon(Try as I may, I am unable to explain), by Surendra Verma in 1989, Jinnay Lahor Nahi Vekhya (One who has not seen Lahore) by Habib Sahib in 1991, other major works Jang ab nahi hogi was performed in 2002 I Karachi by a Indian director Rati Bartholomew, the performences in Chennai 2004 and then in Krachi in 2005 directed by indian director for Tehirk-e-Niswan and Dukh Darya,one of the latest play it is coproduction in one way it is based on the true story of Shehnaz a resident of Pakistani part of Kashmir, accused of being infertile.[20] All these activity related to different issues of India-Pakistan like women, partition, war, culture, human rights and many other that can bring people toghter on a singal platform.

Cricket Diplomacy

Cricket has been an important element in the process of improving relations between India and Pakistan, and improvement have certainly been needed. When it comes to India-Pakistan cricket relations, it begines to signify different meanings and convey different massages to different people like: nationalism, communalism, war, infiltration, insurgency, terrorism, diplomacy, peace,election,cultural exchange, commerical boom, cricketing conflict and so on. Interstingly, it was cricket that formed he first bilateral exchanges in 1952 when Pakistan, led by Abdual Hafeez Kardar, toured India. The first test series was played in 1951-52 when Pakistani team went to India and in 1954-55 Indian team came to Pakistan to play cricket. But from 1961-78 and between 1990-1999, no match was played due to political bad blood. Then should we make the point that cricket has the capacity to break the political jinx?[21] The most glaring example of this attitude is Shaharyar M. Khan, the chairman of Pakistan cricket board writing his classic Cricket: A Bridge of Peace, which throws light on his experience as a manager of the Pakistan's cricket team toure of India in 1999 acknowledged at the outset:

"I had not intended to publish my impression until the unexpectedly warm welcome by the people of India to the enemy team. Their enthusiastic response planted the seed in my mind that cricket's vast untapped energy could be haranessed for understanding and tolerance...After a lifetime in diplomacy, attempting, most unsuccessfully, to overcome tensions, hostility and conflict, I realized cricket could act as bridge of peace."[22]

The higher political leadership also goes to stadiums if both countries are playing with each other and buck up their respective teams. Imran Khan, the legendary Pakistani cricketer, too argued: 'when two countries are triying to become friendly, cricket plays a healing role, cricket becomes a cement in bonding the countries toghter.'[23] Saba karim's comment is perhaps most revealing in this context: 'When the relations between two nations is strained, sportspersons can act as ambassadors and go long way to heal the rifts.'[24] It was thus obvious that the toure had a political dimension as teams played in an emerging climate of rapproachement and peace. Even Colin Powell, the US Secretary of State, on his visit to India during the serise in March 2003, expressed the hope that the enthusiasm generated by the revival oc cricketing ties would certainly have a positive impact on bilateral peace process.[25] Manifestly, emotions run high in cricketing encounters between India and Pakistan. But the fund of mutual goodwill and friendship out there proved sufficient to handle these emotions ensuring that mutual trust and reciprocal faith have come back at least in Indo-Pak cricketing relations. This play is taken as a means to promote bilateral ties between the two countries and bringing the people closer. It is expected that India shall allow common people from Pakistan to visit India to watch the match in its stadiums or play grounds and would grant visas to about thousand Pakistani. This is a positive sign to bring peace and harmony between the two nations.

Pilgrimages Visits:

Every year thousands of pilgrims from both sides visits there holy religious places that attached people of the two rival states and governments of the both the states respect faith of those piligrims. In this way Pakistan governments move forward in renovation of Hindu temples at Ketas sends a positive signal and announce that "We want make Ketas a major tourist attraction. Two million people go to Pushkar every year. We want to bring a million piligrims from India to Ketas. If not a million, at least 5 lakhs", it was a grand project of Musharraf of building a new image for Pakistan as a modern Islamic state that provides space for all religions, including Hindusim.[26] Like millions of Muslim pilgrims came to India from Pakistan and thousand of Sikh pilgrims came to Pakistan from India to pray at their holy places in Rajashtan in India and in Punjab Province of Pakistan by a special train service named Samjhota Express and both of the government welcomes them and shows hospitality and they went back with enchanting memories.[27]

Role of POP Music and Ghazal:

In the Baltistan Movement of the western Himalayas, pop versions of the traditional Arabic, Persian, or Urdu sung in the vernacular Tibetan dialect seem to have acquired a political power by innocuously expressing local political resistance against the nation states of India and Pakistan.[28] What makes this comparatively small Himalayan community especially interesting is its blend of Shi'ite and Tibetan culture and the way the pop ghazals transcend the Indo-Pak border today. Before Partition, Baltistan and Ladakh constituted especially an administrative area in the princely state of Jammu and Kashmir called Ladakh Wazarat. As a result of the Gilgit Rebellion in 1947 Ladakh Wazarat, and therefore also the Balti community, was divided by the Line of Control(LOC) between India and Pakistan.

The Balti people are generally of the Shi'ite faith but the vernacular languagespeak they speak is a Tibetan dialect, and many of the cultural traditions have a strong Tibetean influence. As with other communities on the margins of Indian and Pakistani ethnicity, religious affiliation and identity were politicized in order to access state controlled development resources and in the struggle for local autonomy. Chitral's, most popular band, The Nobles, Marsden demonstrates how the band's khowari-language music develops a local style of Islam to contest the religious and cultural homogenization of postcolnial nationalism in Pakistan. As a target for postcolonial intergrative policies, the Balti communnity is facing a similar dilemma that is further complicated by the community's spread across both sides of the Indo-Pak border.[29] It was the beginning of the twenty first century that Balti activists in Kargil and Nubra started to produce the first Balti pop ghazals. It was a new phenomenon in the Balti community but as a genre of music the pop ghazal was already well established in contemporary South Asian pop music. As I will discuss in more detail below, this development is directly related to the small scale cassette production industry that emerged all over the subcontinent.

By the end of the eighteenth century Urdu ghazal had become very popular in India. It developed its own distinct character, and seemed to capture the imagination of all strands of people irrespective off religious faith. The pop ghazal is unquestionably the most popular from today and can be heared blaring out of the sound system of shops lining local bazaars. The popularity of the ghazal can also be traced to its appropriation by bollywood films and Indian television serials, where it has provided a respectable symbolic form of intimate romantic and even erotic interaction between characters. The most common theme of the ghazal, however, is that unrequited love. In modern times, the ghazal has always been quick to find itself at home with new forms of mass media when the Indian movie industry established itself as the main platform for popular music in the mid twentieth century, the ghazal soon became one of its stock musical formats. More recently, the ghazal established itself on the web. A search on YouTube.com will return severl thousand of hits. The increased availability and low cost of personal computers, broadband access, and the rise of websites like the aforementioned You Tube, as well as social sites like Facebook, make up the infrastructure of a mediascape. In this way footage of incidents such as roits or large scale disasters and accidents, politicaly radical songs and texts, as well as banned or pirated movies, music, and books can still be distributed, not only via computer but also by mobile phones.[30]

Civil Society and Peace Activists

Indo-Pakistan engagement has taken place in multiple phases. In the first phase, from 1947, to the mid 1980's, the two governments were the principle actors, they talked for peace but remained ever ready for war and, indeed, actively clashed four times. In the second phase, from mid 1980's to mid 1990's, sections of the intelligentsia in both India and Pakistan start working for peace. In the third phase people of India became active. They voted for peace for their feet. In the process, they built such immense pressure on the two governments as to leave them little option but to establish and then go forward with the process of peace. Numerous groups have been engaged in promoting Indo-Pak friendship. Some of these groups are:

Pakistan-India People's forum for Peace & Democracy (PIPFPD), Association of Peoples of Asia(APA), Women in Security conflict Management and Peace(WISCOMP), South Asian Forum of Human Rights(SAFHR), Pakistan Peace Coalition and the coalition for Nuclear Disarmament and Peace(CNDP) and India Pakistan Soldiers Initiative for Peace(IPSI),South Asian Free Media Association (SAFMA), Pakistan, Green circle Organization (GCO), Pakistan, Institute for Secular Studies and Peace (ISSP), Pakistan and Aman Ki Asha (Hope for Peace) and a joint venture of two daily newspapers of India and Pakistan. GCO has launched a project where they take citizens of one country to their homes in another country which they left behind after partition in 1947. The people went back to meet their neighbors, their families and to see their homes where they had spent life in the early days of their lives. ISSP has launched a signature campaign in Pakistan to have soft visa procedures for the people of both countries. They gather twenty two thousand (22,000) signatures which they collected from ordinary people of the Pakistan at different schools and colleges and from the public bus stations. Aman Ki Asha (Hope for Peace) is a joint venture of Daily Jang Group, Pakistan and The Times of India which was launched in 2010. The initiative was the outcome of the struggles made by an within programme launched many small projects to promote peace between two nations along with an anthem which says, There are peace activists, human rights organizations and activists, individuals, journalists, scholars, historians, academicians who are all advocating for better ties between India and Pakistan.[31]

Educational Cooperation

India and Pakistan can do much in the educational sector also. Most of the students of South Asian countries go to West for higher foreign education. This involves lots of money and immigration problems along with the chances of militancy and terrorism in the host countries, and because of this factor the visa process is quite complicated and strict for Asian students. So both countries can have bilateral process for educational cooperation and should learn the positive things from each other. This would reduce the economic pressure on the students seeking admission in West and they would be better adjusted due to the somewhat similarity of cultures and languages.[32]

Reality Shows making bridge on gulf between India-Pakistan:

For decades, archenemies India and Pakistan have engaged in dangerous nuclear armes race. Now they are also competing in more cheerful forum. The fractious neighbours are going head to head in a pair of TV reality shows that pit chefs and musicians against each other. Producers hope to contests will help bridge the gulf between two nations that were born from the same womb and have been at each other's throats ever since. There is a significant overlap in the cuisines of both countries, as there is in Language, music and culture. Pakistanis and Indians both love curry, kebab and biryani a spiced rice dish. But they often use different dishes can also vary from one region to another with in the same country. Many Pakistani and Indian have missed out on enjoying the varied tastes of the other country because mutual enmity has made cross border travel difficult. Like food music can also unite people across borders and bring them closer together. Therefore reality shows on TV provide platform for both countries to make a bond of love and peace in the mind of the people of both nations and it really works to make bridge.[33]

Relations in 21st century/ Latest Interventions

Present day saw the decrease in tensions because of the role the civil society, human rights activists, scholars, artists (actors and singers) has brought in towards each other and is paving the way for a peaceful and democratic relationship between the two countries. The both countries are relaxing the visas for its citizens making it convenient for the masses to meet each other often and releasing the prisoners from jails of the opponent countries. President of Pakistan Mr. Asif Ali Zardari visited India on a private visit to Azmir Sharif on April 08, 2012. He was accompanied by his children and had a lunch with the Prime Minsiter of India Mr. Manmohan Singh enroute to the Holy shrine of Salim Chistie a sufi poet and religious scholar of Mughal era. The President of Pakistan invited Indian Prime Minister to visit Pakistan which he accepted and said that he would soon visit Pakistan. They discussed the opportunities for mutual respect, harmony and peace for the betterment of the region and its citizens. After the announcement of most favoured nation by Pakistan to India and softening of trade ties and relaxing the visa process for ordinary men, the Indian cinema made a film EK THA TIGER (once there was a Tiger), 2012 in which the Indian boy from Raw falls in love with a Pakistani girl of ISI and they both eloped betraying the government rivalry of each other but outliving their love for each other as seen between the common people of both countries. The common man of the countries has blood relations, friends and colleagues from both sides and do not have only hostility between them, but they await each other on occasions of marriages, festivals and rituals.

Most of the TV music shows now have both country representatives as the judges and the competitors are also from both countries, even in one music TV show there is a Bangladeshi singer as judge also along with the judges from Pakistan and India. Till this day, we found many Pakistani artists working for Indian films and music industry. To name a few, Rahat Fateh Ali Khan-a Pakistani singer is considered as a success symbol for films in India these days. Some female Pakistani artists are also working in Indian films but due to the difference in cultural norms only woman bold enough would agree to be part of Indian cinema as they have to face the fundamentalists Muslims back in their home country. On the occasion of last Eid after the Holy month of Ramazan, the Muslims of a small town of Joshimath in the state of Uttarakhand, India offered prayers in a Gurdwara by getting permission from the manager of the Goffer the prayers in the open ground so they asked the manager of nearby Gurdwara who whole heartedly allowed them to offer their prayers there, as reported by the News International August, 22, 2012 and The Indian times, August 23, 2012, thus setting an example of cultural harmony and peace.

Suggestions to promote Peace and Harmony between two countries

- The media can bring the people close and create harmony between two nations. The media of both countries can play an effective role by objectively presenting the news and Pakistan and India should start educational ties and offer scholarships for the students of each country and should invite the scholars to come and visit each other and do researches on common interests.
- The literature and syllabus books should not contain hatred to each other and both governments should revise and rewrite the history without depicting hostility to each other.
- There should be cultural exchange programs between India and Pakistan. The artists programs and films and there should be know the Indian Cultural traditions and values.

- Pakistan should invite and take help from the film makers and singers of India to boost its film industry. There should be inter-cultural dialogue between the activists, students, writers, scholars, historians to promote peace and harmony between two nations.
- Trade shall certainly bring the two countries together but visa for common man to visit noteworthy that both countries are also relaxing visas for group tourists to each other country, that is also a good step towards better mutual relationships.
- Cricket should be used to create congenial atmosphere between people of two nations and the leadership should show respect and tolerance towards the defeated side of the country to promote peace in the region.

India and Pakistan share borders, share history, share the heritage, share the sky to say it poetically, so there should be congenial relationship between two countries and it is not always wise to hurl abuse at the neighbour, it should be met with revulsion by all intellectual and learned citizens of these countries who can motivate the stat actors to open hands for a peaceful and democratic relationship between the two nations. We wish for more positive and friendly relationship between India and Pakistan in the coming years.

Footnotes

1. Sheema Kirmani, "Crossing Borders through the Performing Arts", Smitu Khothari,Zia Mian and others, Bridging Partition,Peoples Inititiatives for Peace between India and Pakistan, Orient BlackSwan, New Delhi,2010,p.274.
2. V.P. Malik, Rajender Nath(ed.), Musharraf's War: Foreword, Strategic Research Center, Chandigarh, p 249.
3. Muhammad Ibrar Mohmand, "Pakistan's Cultural Diplomacy with India", at <http://www.
4. A.G. Noorani, "Chasing the Vision", frontline, June 15, 2012, p.88.
5. The Tribune, 23 August, 2012.
6. Nirupama Dutt, "Jottings by an Original Lahoran", Smitu Khothari,Zia Mian and others, Bridging Partition,Peoples Inititiatives for Peace between India and Pakistan, Orient BlackSwan, New Delhi,2010,p.250.
7. Ibid, p.255.
8. Ibid,p.256.
9. Ibid,p.257.

10. Lalita Ramdas, "Dismantling Prejudice: The Challenges For Education", Smitu Khothari,Zia Mian and others, Bridging Partition,Peoples Inititiatives for Peace between India and Pakistan, Orient BlackSwan, New Delhi,2010,p.198.
11. Engineer, Asghar Ali, The Pakistani Text Books and Hatred against India, Institue of Islamic Studies and Study of Society and Secularism, Mumbai, 2000.112.
12. Muhammad Ibrar Mohmand, "Pakistan's Cultural Diplomacy with India", at <http://www.
13. Narendra Panjwani, "India-Pakistan Relations in the Context of Cinema's Hindustan", Smitu Khothari,Zia Mian and others, Bridging Partition,Peoples Inititiatives for Peace between India and Pakistan, Orient BlackSwan, New Delhi,2010,p.266.
14. Ibid,p.269.
15. Ibid,p.271.
16. Muhammad Ibrar Mohmand, "Pakistan's Cultural Diplomacy with India", at http://www. culturaldiplomacy.org
17. Sheema Kirmani, "Crossing Borders through the Performing Arts", Smitu Khothari,Zia Mian and others, Bridging Partition,Peoples Inititiatives for Peace between India and Pakistan, Orient BlackSwan, New Delhi,2010,p.274.
18. Ibid,p.275.
19. Ibid, p.276.
20. Madeeha Gauhar, "Changing Hearts through Theatre", Smitu Khothari,Zia Mian and others, Bridging Partition,Peoples Inititiatives for Peace between India and Pakistan, Orient BlackSwan, New Delhi,2010,p.286.
21. Kausik Bandyopadhyay, "Feel Good, Goodwill and India's Friendship Tour of Pakistan, 2004: Cricket, Ploitics and Diplomacy in Twenty-First-Century India", The International Journal of History of Sports, vol.25, no.12, October 2008, p.1658.
22. Shaharyar Khan, Cricket: A Bridge of Peace, Oxford University Press, New Delhi, 2005, p.7.
23. The Statesman, 11 March 2004, p.12.
24. The Statesman, 25 February 2004, p.13.
25. Ananda Bazar Patrika, 18 March 2004.
26. www.thehindu.com
27. Pakistan Today, 11 April,2012.
28. Jan Magnusson, "The Baltistan Movement and the Power of Pop Ghazals", Asian Ethnology, Vol. 70, no. 1, 2011, p.34.

29. Ibid, p.35.
30. Ibid, p.39.
31. Mubashir Hasan, "The Pakistan-India Peace Process", cited in Simtu Kothari, Zia Man(eds.) and et.al, Bridging Partition People's Initiatives for Peace between India and Pakistan, Orient Blackswan, New Delhi, 2010, pp.20.
32. A. Gupta, "Indias soft Power", Indian Foreign Affairs Journal, Raj Press, New Delhi, 2006, pp.50-52.
33. www.huffingtonpost.com

6

Conclusion

nsecure Pakistan in the backdrop of the US withdrawal from Afghanistan is faced with the twin dilemma of international marginalization as part of fast receding regional relevance and political and economic instability. These fears are heightened by India's rapidly developing economy, political stability and fast paced modernization of its armed forces. For Pakistani fed on the belief, as Christian Fair puts it 'accepting the status quo with India is a defeat', such a scenario is an anathema that it is loathe to accept. This ideological perspective remains the driver that is forcing the Pakistani army in taking calculated military risks as a manifestation of its continued struggle which it must continue and persevere. According to Fair this behaviour of Pakistan is a result of it being fundamentally a dissatisfied state which seeks to increase its prestige through spread of its ideology and religion in pursuit of its revisionist policies.

Why Continued Firing along the LoC?

Within the above backdrop the firing along the LoC has three possible manifestations. At one level it is an attempt to keep the pressure on Kashmir and create insecurity along the border by the combined nexus of Pakistan army, ISI, the terrorists under the United Jihad Council (UJC) supported by the separatists in the J&K. The aim is to keep the status quo in flux. By putting stories of great efforts by the Pakistani army to thwart Indian security forces nefarious designs, an attempt is being made at national mobilisation. It is also to gain public sympathy and support for the army providing it greater flexibility in the flawed civil-military relations. In short, it is an orchestrated plan to provoke India. The Pakistani army believes that it can take such a risk of escalation in the back drop of its effective nuclear capability.Second is the "K" factor. Over the last few years there has been a perceptible decline in militancy and cross border terrorism. Kashmiri separatist leaders like Syed Ali Shah Geelani are too old and Mirwaiz Umar Farookh too weak to sustain the so called separatist struggle. Other leaders like, Yasin malik and Shabir Shah are attempting to pick the gauntlet but have yet to establish their credibility.It is in this milieu that Pakistan is now trying to revamp its entire apparatus in the Kashmir valley, with eye on the forthcoming elections (likely to be postponed to Mar-Apr 2015 owing to floods). This is being done by attempting to induct nearly 1000 militant cadres, reported to be waiting to infiltrate across the LoC. What is worrisome for Pakistani is that militancy and terrorist strikes are not providing any tangible results, or attempts to exploit post-floods anger working.

In the last one month alone nearly 17 terrorists have been killed in the Kashmir Valley (including dozen of them attempting to cross the LoC). In addition, owing to effective counter infiltration and terrorism operations over the last one year there is no worthwhile terrorist leadership left in the valley capable of leading disruption of impending polls or spread antipathy and instigate civil strife during the forthcoming months. Thus it has become an imperative to induct and embed terrorist leadership before the onset of winters.

Interestingly, attempts at infiltration in North and South Kashmir, traditional focus of infiltration has been far and few. There appear to be two reasons: one, Pakistan does not want to be seen as disrupting the flood relief work in the valley, something which could become potential source of alienation and second, vulnerability of its lines of communication should India resorts to massive retaliation. For these apparent reasons the focus of Pakistani firing and escalation has shifted to South of Pir Panjal.

As a result Pakistani firing is largely concentrated on traditional areas of Rajouri and Punch as also across the International Border that includes sectors such as Sambha, Rabirsinghpura, and Chicken's Neck in Akhnoor, etc. Pakistan's increase in intensity and firing on civilian positions both along the border and around is part of an orchestrated strategy aimed at provoking India to relocate civilians to depth areas thereby facilitating infiltration. Locations of cross border tunnel are proofs of Pakistan's nefarious designs.

Third is the impending election in J&K. Successful elections which could throw up electoral arithmetic in which centrist forces become powerful power brokers would result in a government that would follow strong nationalist policies thus severely curbing the separatist space. The manner in which India reacted to the Huriyat leaders meeting Pakistan's High

Commissioner should have made absolutely clear to Islamabad that New Delhi with growing international support will brook little or no dissidence from these groups operating outside the constitutional process.

Apart from above factors, it appears that Pakistani military is attempting at brinkmanship to bring the beleaguered country back into global relevance by focusing on Kashmir (the forgotten dispute) especially now with the focus shifting to the ISIS.

India's Response

India needs to follow a three pronged strategy: First, a swift, sharp and effective response backed by controlled escalation to Pakistan's provocations. India should be in no doubt that Pakistan could attempt at escalation misreading Indian resolve. Second, India should expose Pakistan's crass attempts to rake up tensions in the subcontinent by adequately exposing its nefarious designs both in Kashmir and rest of the country. There should be no talks till such time Pakistan mends its ways and agrees to meaningful dialogue. Third, Kashmir post-flood reconstruction work must gain momentum and fair distribution. The state administration must be encouraged to show empathy in distribution of relief.Time has also come for another round of dialogue with all shades of opinion in Kashmir including separatist leadership but strictly within the confines of the Indian constitution. In so far as dialogue with Pakistan is concerned it should be made clear that India wants peace but will not bow down to such provocations.

The India-Pakistan Relations is one of the most complex bilateral relations in the world. Innumerable factors design to push this bilateral ties on the boiling pot. The nefarious colonial designs and weak internal political will invariably create problems in identifying simple solutions of the lingering issues. In historical perspective it is clear that India and Pakistan is the core states of South Asia which are culturally similar linguistically unite geographically closed and historically related. But it is strange that despite the geographical, historical and cultural similarity the relations between these two states not so much smooth and peaceful. The demand for Pakistan was itself based on distrust. Roots of this kind of relationship between India-Pakistan can be seen in the colonial history of Indian subcontinent. British colonial rules established a tradition by the partition of this subcontinent that creates a chain of struggles, disputes and instability in the region. Bilateral relations between India and Pakistan are undoubtedly the most important in South Asia and the world also. But relations among both states not at all smooth in nature and has been full of ups and downs. Now the both countries are overtly nuclear powered, they poses greater risk, if the ongoing crisis is not resolved. Difficulties in their relations arise mainly because their differences are not rooted in legal and constitutional interpretations and misunderstanding, but in geography, emotional legacies past history and their divergent views on the doctrine of two - nation theory. The leaders of the both the states are responsible for creating this kind of psyche, which cause the differences.

It has resulted from a number of complex factors like legacy, the difference in religion and race, conflicting national interests, ideologies, power struggle. From the very beginning, the two powers became involved in a conflict ridden relationship over the status of the former princely -state of Jammu and Kashmir and forced immigrate of thousands of Hindu and Muslim into the new countries which affected both emerging countries. The dispute has proved severely opposed to resolution because, at bottom, it is infused with the self-images of the two states. Pakistan deemed its identity as a Muslim homeland incomplete without Kashmir; while India sees its control over this Muslim-majority state as a demonstration of its secular identification. This tense relationship has resulted in three major wars (1947-48, 1965, 1971) and a limited one (1999) and multiple crises like the question of minorities, evacuee property, sharing of assert, division of military stores, Hadrabad and Junagarh --- the list is endless. A number of promising agreements were made. Further , the Tashkent and Shimla, agreements and Lahor declaration. Although they resolved the Indus Waters dispute in 1960 and the Rann of Kutch dispute in 1968 through negotiations, there was no agreed mechanism to guide their stable conflictual relationship. After 1971, consequent the liberation of East Pakistan and formation of Bangladesh, India gained legitimate status of being an emerging power in South Asia. In the 1980s the two sides began to talk on the Siachen, Sir Creek and the Tulbul-Wullar disputes and put in place a series of confidence building measures pertaining to conventional and nuclear weapons power. These negotiations had no set time table and were held on a need to meet basis. There was no compulsion on either side to continue their negotiations when their relationship declined in the face of terrorist attack or armed aggression.Peace and stability are pre-requisites for economic development, trade and politico-socio-cultural relations. This has assumed added urgency since South Asia has obtained nuclear capability, as there is now little margin for error. It is imperative that the security situation in South Asia is stabilised and made as resistant as possible to the periodic shocks caused by the actions of NSAs. Avoidance of crises, prevention of conflicts and the building of mutual confidence should therefore be common objectives for the two countries.

There is a huge potential for the expansion of bilateral trade between India and Pakistan, especially now that the long-standing issue of Pakistan granting Most Favoured Nation status to India seems closer than ever to being resolved. But other issues, such as non-tariff barriers to trade, will have to be addressed before any positive move can be made towards increasing trade. There is also a long list of items on the negative list which have to be looked at before significant improvement can be achieved. The promotion of official trade will discourage smuggling and other means of illegal trade that at present cost the two countries substantial lost revenue.

The peace process launched in January 2004 had been one of the most productive and sustained in the history of a dismal bilateral relationship. This process has seen significant expansion of bilateral trade, improved people to people contact, a ceasefire on their borders, the implementation of number of confidence-building measures in disputed Kashmir, and above all serious back channel negotiation on the Kashmir question. While its policy makers have increasingly talked about the urgent need to construct a 'peaceful periphery' for many of its leader an integrated northwest region of the subcontinent was a living memory. None exemplifies this better than Prime Minister Man Mohan Singh of India, who's family lived in the north west part of what is now Pakistan and migrated to India after partition. In early 2007, speaking on India's relations with its neighbors, Singh mused on his aspirations for restoring these historic connections:

"I sincerely believe... that the destiny of the people of South Asia is interlinked. It is not just our past that links us, but our future too. India cannot be a prosperous, dynamic economy and a stable polity if our neighborhood as a whole is also not economically prosperous and politically stable. Similarly, our neighbors cannot prosper if India does not do so as well. There are enormous opportunities for promoting mutually beneficial cooperation in South Asia. To exploit these opportunities, the nations of South Asia have to work sincerely to control the scourge of terrorism and extremism... I dream of a day, while retaining our respective national identities, one can have breakfast in Amritsar, lunch in Lahore and dinner in Kabul. That is how my forefathers lived. That is how I want to our grandchildren to live."

Today, more than sixty five years after independence, the common people as well as the elite of India and Pakistan are concerning towards establishing condition for permanent peace. But unfortunately the situation is not so much better for India and Pakistan which it should be but the power of the old mindset is declining and the momentum for peace is growing.

Regarding the development of the nuclear policies of the two countries both have adopted a policy of minimum deterrence. Though this did not deter the two states from clashing for instance the Kargil War and nuclear race is going on but is has also been realized by both the countries that the probability of using the nuclear force against the other is little. Here it is pertinent to mention that if nuclear force is used it would be disastrous for both the countries. In the last decade of this century it was accepted that both India and Pakistan had a nuclear military capability. The nuclear tests had the following repercussion on the relations of India and Pakistan:

- India and Pakistan both started liking at each other with suspicion and mutual distrust.
- Both countries started blaming each other for real or imaginary bad conduct and the mutual co-operation came down to a very low level.
- Both the nations started spending more on the deals on defense.

The nuclear explosion of 1998 proved to the world that Pakistan's policy is reactive and dubious. The result was the Lahore Bus Diplomacy between India and Pakistan could not show any positive result as Pakistan indirectly imposed the Kargil strife on India. The whole world condemned this action of Pakistan. Though India won the strife in the ends at a very heavy cost, but the relations between the two countries became strained again. India and Pakistan have been living dangerously with their current strategies for security through an arms race since independence. Arms race has increased the threat perception towards each other and has affected adversely the development process. It is time to consider seriously the alternatives for solving the problems. It is time for transition from power politics and traditional forms of dispute resolution to national problem and to discovery of mutually beneficial options. Overt nuclear capability of these nations has highlighted the need for greater co-operation. Therefore the time has come with the advance thinking in Indo-Pak relations on the issues like security and development. They should have to arrange more and more dialogues discussions and interactions with open mind for some fruitful solutions. These measures will reduce the tensions between both the countries generated by nuclear and missile programmes. Since 2001, the two nations are moving with the global trend for peace and security. This is evident that war remained the only option for so long and none of the conflicting parties have been able to settle the issues in its favour. Therefore it is only logical and practical to try another option i.e. peace through dialogue for solving the problem.

Pakistan and India share the same and common cultural history, food, language, dress and are tied with the upheaval of the invaders and colonial powers of the past as well. There cannot be two more similar people in other areas of the world. As it was Muslims from whom the Britain took charge. Both countries blame each other for all the massacre and destruction caused at the time of partition and do not realize that the same incidents were found on both sides. The citizens of both countries remain strongly interrelated and interconnected with each other through the similar culture, weathers, festivities and traditions which are bonding them together despite the diplomatic differences promoted by the states. The Social and cultural relationship with Pakistan is also an area which matters to concerns the emotions and belief of a common man. Similar people with common history can be the biggest enemies because the hurt of a perceived betrayal is the most. Emotion rules over the reason. Minorities of the both nations like Hindus in Pakistan and Muslims in India are still not mingled up and attached with the society in which they live. Although India is socially, politically and economically better than Pakistan and had made remarkable progress in all spheres as compared to Pakistan, but the cultural relationship in term of literature, cricket, pilgrimage and education, media, theater, cinema will surely help to improve the confidence for ties for the future.

The 1999 Lahore Memorandum of Understanding was the first Ind-Pakistan effort to come to grips with their mutual problems and to explore measures to reduce tensions in a nuclearised South Asia. Though the process was interrupted by the Kargil episode, the proposed confidence-building measures (CBMs) were taken up when the composite dialogue resumed in 2004, resulting in some significant bilateral agreements. It appears, however, that the list of CBMs agreed to at Lahore has been exhausted and currently there seems to be no discernible forward movement in the bilateral talks. It is important that negotiators think of new and innovative CBMs and establish an oversight and review mechanism to monitor the performance of past agreements, to give some impetus to the peace process. But CBMs can only be expected to provide temporary stability at best and, ultimately, the two countries' outstanding political problems, including the Kashmir dispute, will need to be resolved. The efforts at building confidence and trust and seeking resolution of disputes can only bear fruit if the process is sustained and remains uninterrupted. On many occasions in the recent past, certain groups and individuals opposed to reconciliation between India and Pakistan have succeeded in disrupting the peace efforts. The two countries will have to resist these disruptive forces by evolving institutional mechanisms to deal with them. Past efforts were half-hearted and depended to a large extent on the character and attitudes of the individuals representing the two countries in the Joint Counter-terrorism mechanism. As the conflict in Afghanistan winds down, India and Pakistan will need to discuss their respective legitimate interests in that country. India will need to convince Pakistan that its interest in Afghanistan is not aimed at opening up a new front in the west or promote destabilisation in the two Pakistani provinces bordering Afghanistan. For its part, Pakistan will need to reassure India that it respects the legitimate and sovereign rights of India and Afghanistan to develop their bilateral relations. Due to its geographical position, Pakistan can either facilitate or block the trade between India and Afghanistan passing through its territory, but that will be entirely dependent on the state of India-Pakistan relations.

Suggestions:

The different issues which are providing as hindrance in good relations between two countries are not such, which cannot be resolved through dialogue and mutual understanding. The following measures are suggested which would help to improve cordial relations between the two countries:

- South Asia is home to one-fifth of humanity. Around 20% of world's population lives in this region with plenty of problems and issues like illiteracy, poverty, malnutrition, scarcity of water, unemployment and etc. India and Pakistan peace will help other regional states to overcome their common, specifically, non-traditional problems and issues.
- There is much pressure from the peoples from the India and Pakistan on the two respective governments. The masses on the two sides have changed their stereotyped mindsets after the commencement of the people to people contact. The revival of diplomatic contacts and reopening of their High Commissions have played a greater role in this regard. Exchange of scholars, artists, politicians, educationists and above all common people who are visiting their relatives across

the borders helped the people to overcome threat perception at public level.

- The Composite Dialogue is taking place at a correct time when the whole world is keen to have peace in South Asia. Greater influence and insistence can be felt with regard to international players, especially the USA, EU, China, Japan, Muslim bloc and Russia. South Asia appears to be a high risk conflict zone and has also become a nuclear flashpoint. While considering the necessity or regional peace in South Asia, the global powers fully endorse the settlement of Kashmir issues along with all bilateral differences between India and Pakistan.
- Confidence building measures require a continuing exercise. These measures cannot resolve all the issues but can reduce tensions and improve the regional environment greatly. India-Pakistan dialogue is therefore needed to be kept on track until the two states reach a final resolution or the issues. Existing CBMs in the military field also should be strengthened and improved effectively according to the requirement.
- Interaction between the Chambers of Commerce and Industries of both the states should be encouraged to develop, trade, commerce and industry. The trade normalization process will increase trade opportunities for both India and Pakistan. Even though the automobile sector in Pakistan and the textile sector in India have resisted trade liberalization, there is no rationale for holding back the process which shall inevitably benefit both the countries. India and Pakistan need to work together in several areas to be able to realize the untapped trade potential. So far only incremental steps are being considered by the two governments to improve cross-border movement of goods. A comprehensive and integrated international land transport policy needs to be put in place not only to provide rail and road services connecting the two countries but also linking sea ports through land borders to enable connectivity with the rest of the world as well. India should continue to lower its non-tariff barriers as part of its ongoing reform process. In addition, a more concerted effort needs to be made to facilitate businessmen in overcoming their apprehensions about entering each other's markets and selling their products along with their country labels across the border fearlessly. The unprecedented number of exhibitions and fairs held in India and Pakistan, displaying each other's products, has been met by an overwhelming response from consumers; providing support for such efforts to continue.

- While the removal of restrictions on FDI flows has opened up new investment opportunities, businessmen from India and Pakistan are reluctant to invest due to fear of a possible disruptive political event. Investors also fear becoming easy targets for those who oppose their presence. Businessmen willing to invest could enter into joint ventures without physically locating in each other's territory, as the first step to entry, till legal systems safeguard investments and there is improvement in investors' confidence. For a liberal visa regime to be in place, electronic 'smart systems' should be used to screen visa applications and track physical movement of people, while avoiding undue harassment to genuine traders. Telecommunication channels also need to be opened up to foster people-to-people contact and reduce business costs. The existing communication system between India and Pakistan does not permit travelers to use their mobile phones in the other's country. Buying local SIM (Subscriber Identity Module) cards too is not an easy option, involving a lot of paper work for those travelling. As a result, visitors and businessmen have developed informal mechanisms of procuring local SIM-cards through friends and relatives. The issue of improving telecommunication between the two countries was raised in the 7th round of talks and is expected to be a part of the trade normalization process.
- India and Pakistan need to constantly engage with one another to understand each other's regulatory regimes. As new businessmen enter into trading relations, it is important to have forums that bring buyers and sellers together. Guaranteed payments are essential for building new and lasting business partnerships, for which banking channels would need to be improved. An innovative dispute resolution system should also be put in place. For many years, Dubai has provided as a facilitator for trade and guaranteed payments between India and Pakistan. Thus, a third country wherein India and Pakistan share mutual trust could provide for an effective dispute resolution mechanism. Moreover, it is important for the business communities to create multilevel channels of communication which can reduce misconceptions, bridge information gaps, and generate a significant change in the business environment of the two countries. All such holistic measures could help in realizing the untapped trade potential between India and Pakistan.
- Agro- Climatic conditions being same in both the countries, possibilities for agriculture co-operation should be explored and

enhanced. It will help in attaining food self sufficiency and earning revenue from the other countries.

- The media can bring the people close and create harmony between two nations. The media of both countries can play an effective role by objectively presenting the news and Pakistan and India should start educational ties and offer scholarships for the students of each country and should invite the scholars to come and visit each other and do researches on common interests.
- The literature and syllabus books should not contain hatred to each other and both governments should revise and rewrite the history without depicting hostility to each other.
- There should be cultural exchange programs between India and Pakistan. The artists programs and films and there should be know the Indian Cultural traditions and values.
- Pakistan should invite and take help from the film makers and singers of India to boost its film industry. There should be inter-cultural dialogue between the activists, students, writers, scholars, historians to promote peace and harmony between two nations.
- Cricket should be used to create congenial atmosphere between people of two nations and the leadership should show respect and tolerance towards the defeated side of the country to promote peace in the region.
- Intelligence agencies of both the nations should not blame each other for their internal disturbances. Transparency on defense policy issues and equipments is required to create cordial atmosphere in both the countries. Initially it could be done simply by providing the information about the military affairs, such as equipment holding and weapon acquisitions after the event. The possibilities of collective non military activities between military personal in both the nations should be explored.
- People of both countries are always enthusiastic to visit the territory of each other so both countries should offer attractive incentives from tourism point of view. It will help in developing harmonious relations on the one hand in both nations and on the other hand it will give boost to the revenue for these two states.
- Simplification in the procedure for granting for granting visa is required on priority basis. Visitors coming from both the countries help in developing the atmosphere for peace and fairs and Festivals

should be organized collectively by both the states to spread the message of harmony, peace and mutual trust and faith.

Last but not least, Joint ventures between the two countries are non-existent, and so is direct investment. While India and Pakistan compete to sell their goods in the global market, there are many areas of enterprise in which both the countries can complement each other's needs and hence produce cost- effective, quality goods. Potential sectors for joint ventures include agricultural products, tires, auto spare parts, minerals, chemicals, pharmaceuticals, leather, textile and telecommunications, education and literature sector, media, theatre, cinema, sports, and many others. The exchange of technology and skills between the two neighbors will help enhance the quality of their goods at comparatively cheaper prices. Telecommunication networking between them will help closer interaction between the elite as well as common people. Also joint project to provide IT related services for world markets would be an attractive proposition for global companies. Free intra country tourism will ensure people to people contact. Also, joint tourism projects, especially in the Himalayan region could provide a fillip to the tourism industry in both the countries. India and Pakistan can establish joint ventures to harness and transmit the region's hydropower resources. Cooperation in water management and hydropower projects can help in increasing irrigation benefits, decreasing risks of floods, and establishing Indo-Pakistan electric grid system for intra-country transmission of electricity.

Therefore it can be said that Wars did not resolve any issue in the past. We believed that Kashmir can become the bridge to peace between the two countries, which has so far been the primary cause of hostility between India and Pakistan. The collaboration of civil and military spheres for peace gained legitimacy, needless to say this kind of synergy is only the beginning and needs to be consolidated and further strengthened through a combination of initiatives in the years ahead. Despite all, It was convinced that we were on the wrong track as far as neighborhood management was concerned. We needed a new approach to convert the traditional confrontation and conflict approach to one of cooperation and convergence. People in South Asia, home to a vast majority of the world's poor, need the availability of employment opportunities more than anything else. This is essential so that no one takes interest in destructive activities like terrorism. If there is cooperation between India and Pakistan and not conflict, vast opportunities will open up for trade, travel and development that will create prosperity in both nations.